FIONA DE LONDRAS
MÁIRÉAD ENRIGHT

REPEALING THE 8TH

Reforming Irish abortion law

POLICY PRESS SHORTS POLICY & PRACTICE

First published in Great Britain in 2018 by

Policy Press
University of Bristol
1-9 Old Park Hill
Bristol
BS2 8BB
UK
t: +44 (0)117 954 5940
pp-info@bristol.ac.uk
www.policypress.co.uk

North America office:
Policy Press
c/o The University of Chicago Press
1427 East 60th Street
Chicago, IL 60637, USA
t: +1 773 702 7700
f: +1 773 702 9756
sales@press.uchicago.edu
www.press.uchicago.edu

British Library Cataloguing in Publication Data
A catalogue record for this book is available from the British Library.

Library of Congress Cataloging-in-Publication Data
A catalog record for this book has been requested.

ISBN 978-1-4473-4751-4 (hardback)
ISBN 978-1-4473-4752-1 (ePub)
ISBN 978-1-4473-4753-8 (Mobi)
ISBN 978-1-4473-4754-5 (OA PDF)

Cover design by Policy Press
Front cover: image kindly supplied by Aoife Hamill
Printed and bound in Great Britain by CMP, Poole
Policy Press uses environmentally responsible print partners

Contents

Acknowledgements

We are grateful to the College of Arts and Law, University of Birmingham and Birmingham Law School, which supported us in making this book freely available to the public through Open Access publishing; particular thanks to Sheena Robertson, Professor Michael Whitby, Professor Joanna Gray and Dr Sophie Boyron for endorsing (and funding) the project.

Our thanks go also to Magdalena Furgalska for her research assistance, Victoria Pittman and her team at Policy Press, and the many dozens of activists, academics, friends, abortion service providers, abortion care seekers and politicians with whom we have discussed the issues canvassed here over the years. Particular thanks to Bríd ní Ghráinne, Christine Ryan, Aisling McMahon, Sinead McEneaney, Laura Cahillane and Sandra Duffy for reading and commenting on parts of the manuscript despite the very short turnaround. All opinions, errors and omissions are ours.

The draft legislation we propose in Chapter 5 is in many senses the result of a long process of collective feminist deliberation. It was informed by earlier drafting exercises and discussions with Vicky Conway, Mary Donnelly, Ruth Fletcher, Natalie McDonnell, Sheelagh McGuinness, Kathryn McNeilly, Claire Murray, Sinead Ring and Sorcha uí Chonnachtaigh. Leah Hoctor, Maeve Taylor, Sally Sheldon, Julie McCandless, Sheelagh McGuinness, Aoife Nolan, Deirdre Duffy, Joanna Erdman and Catherine O'Rourke provided helpful comments on previous such drafts.

The manuscript was completed on 15 November 2017 and the law is accurate as of that date.

A note on terminology

Throughout this text we use the terms pregnant person/s, pregnant women, pregnant woman, pregnant people, woman, and women interchangeably. We recognise that many trans* and non-binary people can become pregnant and may need abortion care. In all instances, we include all those who may seek and need abortion care within these terms.

1

The case for repealing the 8th

The 8th Amendment to the Irish Constitution was ratified in 1983,[1] and provides—in the form of Article 40.3.3—that:

> The State acknowledges the right to life of the unborn and, with due regard to the equal right to life of the mother, guarantees in its laws to respect, and, as far as practicable, by its laws to defend and vindicate that right.

At first glance, the 8th Amendment may seem innocuous or merely aspirational. However, over time this provision, which could have been read in dozens of ways, has come to ground a near-absolute prohibition on abortion in Irish law.[2]

The 8th Amendment treats the foetus as a constitutional person, separate from the pregnant person to the extent that it is entitled to its own legal representation, and with a right to life exactly equivalent

---

[1] 66.9% of voters voted in support of the 8th Amendment. The turnout was 53.6%.

[2] We are indebted to Ruth Fletcher here. See generally Fletcher, Ruth, 'Judgment: *Attorney General v X*', in Enright, Máiréad et al (eds) *Northern/Irish Feminist Judgments: Judges' Troubles and the Gendered Politics of Identity* (2017, Hart/Bloomsbury Publishing).

to hers.[3] The constitutional concept of 'life' has been interpreted restrictively. Rather than recognise the 8th Amendment as protecting life in all its richness and depth, successive courts and governments have been content to assume that it only protects the bare condition of being alive.[4] Those other rights that confer dignity and meaning on life—rights to privacy, equality, bodily autonomy and so on—have been excised from the law on abortion by prevailing interpretations of the 8th Amendment. The moment we become pregnant, our constitutional rights are subordinated to the right to life of the unborn and circumscribed by the constitutional status of 'mother'.[5] There are two points here. First, the Amendment's concentration on life as mere survival has stripped the 'as far as practicable' clause of the 8th Amendment of its potential to rationalise abortion law and policy in Ireland. If the state's obligation is merely to keep both pregnant person and foetus alive, real questions of practicability—of how much pain, suffering or risk the pregnant person can be compelled to endure—carry no constitutional weight. Ordinary constitutional principles of proportionality do not apply. The only limit is that the state need not do what is 'futile' to preserve foetal life.[6] So the 8th Amendment has provided cover for drastic intrusions into pregnant people's private lives. For example, in the history of the 8th Amendment, people acting 'on behalf of' the unborn have taken cases to disrupt attempts to access abortion care,[7] while state actors have tried to vindicate the right to life of the 'unborn' by attempting to prevent people from travelling for

---

[3] Smyth, Lisa, 'Feminism and Abortion Politics: Choice, Rights, and Reproductive Freedom' (2002) 25(3) *Women's Studies International Forum* 335.

[4] Fletcher, Ruth (see note 2). See also McNeilly, Kathryn, 'From the Right to Life to the Right to Livability: Radically Reapproaching "Life" in Human Rights Politics' (2015) 41(1) *Australian Feminist Law Journal* 141.

[5] Article 40.3.3, Constitution of Ireland.

[6] *Attorney General v X* [1992] 1 IR 1; *PP v HSE* [2014] IEHC 622.

[7] *Attorney General (SPUC) v Open Door Counselling & Well Woman Centre Ltd* [1988] IR 593; *SPUC v Grogan* [1989] IR 753.

abortion,[8] or imposing unwanted medical interventions on women.[9] Second, concentration on mere biological life produces highly artificial legal reasoning. We do not treat two such different entities as a foetus and a grown woman equally when we treat them the same. The law can only achieve this sameness by ruling out all of the considerations that make the pregnant person's life different from that of the foetus, so that a court is simply comparing each one's chance of remaining alive. The Supreme Court has held that when a pregnant person proposes to terminate a pregnancy, the risk of loss of the foetus' life is 100%. So, in order to be entitled to an abortion, the pregnant person must show that the risk that she will die, unless she obtains the abortion, is substantively as great.[10] Of course, this will almost never be the case.

This approach to the 8th Amendment was not inevitable, but it was intended.[11] The 8th Amendment was not legally necessary; there was no discernible movement to legalise abortion (which was criminalised) in Ireland at the time, and the Supreme Court had made clear that even though there was a limited constitutional right to access contraception this did not extend to a right to access lawful abortion. However, the referendum that led to the 8th Amendment was the product of a potent mix of political turbulence, religious domination and conservative lobbying.[12] It was at once a pre-emptive strike against any further liberation for woman, and a backlash against the limited liberation that had already occurred. Its intention was to ensure that, regardless of

---

[8]   *Attorney General v X* (see note 6).

[9]   Attempts to secure medical treatment in spite of the pregnant woman's lack of consent include *South Western Health Board v K and Anor* [2002] IEHC 104; *Health Service Executive v F* (High Court, *ex tempore,* Birmingham J., 20 November 2010). See also *Mother A v Waterford Regional Hospital* (High Court, Hedigan J., 11 March 2013), in which the pregnant woman ultimately agreed to have a Caesarean section so that the court did not have to reach a decision.

[10]   *Attorney General v X* (see note 6).

[11]   McGuinness, Sheelagh, 'Commentary on *Attorney General v X*', in Enright, Máiréad et al (eds) (see note 2).

[12]   On the campaign, see further Connolly, Linda, *The Irish Women's Movement: From Revolution to Devolution* (2001, Springer), pp 163-168.

societal change and the liberalisation of Irish politics, increased access to lawful abortion would only ever be possible if a successful referendum campaign were run to repeal the 8th Amendment. As we know, achieving that has proven difficult, and since 1983 no referendum has ever been put to the electorate that would have liberalised abortion law in any meaningful sense.

The key judgment on the 8th Amendment is *Attorney General v X*.[13] In that case, the Supreme Court—faced with a suicidal teenager, pregnant through rape and seeking to travel for an abortion—developed the test for entitlement to access an abortion, which is now reflected in the Protection of Life During Pregnancy Act 2013 (PLDPA). Under this test, a pregnant person may only access an abortion where her life, as opposed to her health, is at 'real and substantial risk', including risk from suicide, and that risk may only be avoided by terminating the pregnancy. Because the focus is solely on 'life', if a foetus' life is at risk, the state, and by extension medical personnel, may do anything practicable to save it; her suffering does not make that intervention impracticable or unconstitutional.

Although this limited decision may seem entirely consistent with the desired outcome of the 8th Amendment, *X* was heavily criticised by anti-abortion campaigners.[14] In their view, allowing for abortion in situations of a risk of suicide subverted the intent of the 1983 referendum; instead, pregnant women could be 'minded'[15] so that the pregnancy could be carried to term. Abortion was not necessary; it did not, they continued to argue, 'save lives'. Anti-abortion activists supported referendums (1992 and 2002) attempting to remove the suicide exception from the Constitution. These were unsuccessful.

Abortion travel has been the escape hatch in Ireland's law; crisis pregnancy has always driven Irish women to travel to England

---

[13] See note 6.

[14] See, for example, Binchy, William, 'New Abortion Law Regime will have no Effective Limits', *The Irish Times*, 6 March 1992.

[15] See comments to this effect of Catherine Bannon in Tynan, Maol Muire, 'Campaign to Amend the Constitution Launched', *The Irish Times*, 11 March 1992.

and elsewhere.[16] While the Amendment was still new, the Society for the Protection of the Unborn Child (SPUC) brought cases attacking healthcare providers who assisted women to travel abroad for abortions.[17] In X, the Attorney General sought an injunction to prevent a teenager from travelling for abortion. The majority of the Supreme Court recognised that pregnant people could not be prevented from travelling abroad to access abortions, in part because injunctions restricting travel were too difficult to enforce. Soon after X, the right to travel was added to the Constitution in a referendum, as the 13th Amendment to the Constitution.[18] The 14th Amendment guaranteed a limited right to access the information necessary to obtain an abortion abroad.[19] With the state's reliance on exporting abortion firmly installed in the Constitution, the development of abortion law at home stalled. The government eventually legislated to regulate the provision of information on accessing abortion abroad.[20] However, it did not pass any legislation on access to abortion at home until 2013. The courts have not considered expanding the constitutional abortion law set out in the X case; the few abortion cases since X have largely stayed within the realms of abortion travel for teenagers and applied the X decision without setting out any more comprehensive interpretation of the 8th Amendment.[21]

---

[16] Hug, Chrystel, *The Politics of Sexual Morality in Ireland* (2016, Springer), p 160.

[17] *Attorney General (SPUC) v Open Door Counselling & Well Woman Centre Ltd* [1988] IR 593; *SPUC v Grogan* [1989] IR 753.

[18] Article 40.3.3, Constitution of Ireland.

[19] On the background to these referendums, see further McAvoy, Sandra, 'Vindicating Women's Rights in a Foetocentric State: The Longest Irish journey', in Giffney, Noreen and Shildrick, Margrit (eds) *Theory on the Edge* (2013, Palgrave), p 39.

[20] Access to Information (Services outside the State for Termination of Pregnancy) Act 1995 (Abortion Information Act).

[21] Mary O'Toole, evidence to the Joint Committee on the Eighth Amendment to the Constitution, 25 September 2017, referencing *A and B v EHB and C* [1997] IEHC 176 and *D v HSE* (unreported, High Court, McKechnie J., May 2007).

Irish abortion legislation

It is a crime for anyone, including pregnant people, to provide or access abortion in Ireland, except as a life-saving measure under the PLDPA.[22] Abortion is lawful only if there is a 'real and substantial risk' to the life, as opposed to the health, of the pregnant woman, and if that risk can *only* be averted by termination of the pregnancy.[23] This means that, in most cases, pregnant people who need abortions will not be able to access abortion care in Ireland. The test of 'real and substantial risk' is unclear: the risk to the pregnant person's life need not be immediate or imminent before abortion can be offered.[24] However, the Constitution requires doctors to *wait* until a severe risk to health caused by the pregnancy has clearly turned into a risk to life before offering abortion care. Doctors must undertake both medical and legal analysis at the same time, so that care in pregnancy is provided 'in the shadow of a custodial sentence for both the clinician and the woman'.[25] Thus, in adhering to the Constitution a doctor may be required to place a pregnant patient's long-term health, or life, at active risk before the pregnancy can be terminated. This also means, as we discuss in Chapter 4, that medical practitioners hold immense power under that Act, including power to refuse treatment or delay a decision so that a woman may be unable to access lawful abortion, even if her life is at sufficient risk to 'qualify' under the Act.

Even in life-threatening cases, an abortion is not permitted if the foetus has reached viability.[26] Instead, the baby will be delivered early, and steps may even be taken to maintain the pregnancy until the foetus is viable.[27] One might imagine that if the law requires

---

[22] Section 22, PLDPA 2013.

[23] Sections 7-9, PLDPA 2013.

[24] *Attorney General v X* (see note 6).

[25] Rhona Mahony, evidence to the Joint Committee on the Eighth Amendment to the Constitution, 11 October 2017.

[26] *Attorney General v X* (see note 6); PLDPA 2013.

[27] 'Viability' here is a medical term – it refers to the point at which a foetus can survive outside of the womb, which is affected by multiple factors

viable babies to be delivered, it is less concerned about foetuses that have not yet attained viability. However, that is not the case. Maire Whelan, the Attorney General from 2011 to 2017, maintained that there is no necessary constitutional right to abortion even where the foetus has been diagnosed with a 'fatal foetal abnormality',[28] which means that it will almost certainly not be born alive.[29] Moreover, the legal prohibition on abortion applies irrespective of how advanced the pregnancy is.[30] This also means that the prohibition applies to all forms of abortion; it makes no distinction between surgical and medical abortion (the 'abortion pill').[31]

The PLDPA requires at least two doctors to certify that there is a 'real and substantial risk' to life that can only be averted by ending the pregnancy before abortion can lawfully be offered.[32] Although the constitutional right to access abortion applies equally whether the risk to life is from a physical risk or from a risk to suicide, the Act imposes additional procedural requirements in cases of risk of suicide.[33] Also, apart from in emergencies, medical professionals are entitled to

---

including birthweight and gestational age: Royal College of Obstetricians and Gyneacologists, 'Perinatal Management of Pregnant Women at the Threshold of Infant Viability – The Obstetric Perspective', Scientific Impact Paper No. 41 (2014), available at www.rcog.org.uk/en/guidelines-research-services/guidelines/sip41. See also Fergal Malone, evidence to the Joint Committee on the Eighth Amendment to the Constitution, 11 October 2017.

[28] Given its common vernacular usage in Irish abortion law debates, we use the term 'fatal foetal abnormality' here. However, when discussing future law we prefer 'foetal anomaly', and use this term when writing prospectively in Chapters 4 and 5 in particular.

[29] O'Halloran, Marie, 'Clare Daly Criticises Approach to Fatal Foetal Abnormality Cases', *The Irish Times*, 6 July 2016.

[30] The PLDPLA 2013 makes no reference to gestational limits.

[31] See the definition of 'medical procedure' in s. 2(1), PLDPA 2013. For a general critique of the Act see Taylor, Maeve, 'Women's Right to Health and Ireland's Abortion Laws' (2015) 130(1) *International Journal of Gynaecology and Obstetrics* 93.

[32] Sections 6-8, PLDPA 2013.

[33] Section 8, PLDPA 2013.

refuse abortion care to a pregnant person under the Act if they have a conscientious objection to abortion.[34]

The PLDPA makes no reference to the pregnant woman's wishes or voice. Once she has sought abortion care, all other decisions are made by someone else: by medics, by lawyers, by courts, by 'the system'. In reality, only people with no other choice use the 2013 Act, even if their lives are in danger.[35] Anyone able to do so travels abroad to access an abortion,[36] or imports abortion pills illegally.[37] As we have already seen, the Constitution contains a structural tolerance and expectation of abortion travel, and of access to information about abortion services abroad. The law restricts the publication of abortion information, and constrains medics and pregnancy counsellors in offering assistance.[38] The law anticipates that anyone seeking an abortion abroad must arrange it for themselves.

The current legal regime demonstrates in stark terms just how restrictive the 8th Amendment is. As shown in Chapter 2, even if the Oireachtas wanted to make abortion more widely available, it could not. For that to happen, the Constitution must be changed.

---

[34] Section 17, PLDPA 2013.

[35] Anthony McCarthy, evidence to the Joint Committee on the Eighth Amendment to the Constitution, 8 November 2017.

[36] In 2015, 3,451 women with addresses in the Republic of Ireland accessed abortion under the Abortion Act 1967: Department of Health, *Abortion Statistics, England and Wales: 2015* (2016).

[37] Between 2010 and 2012, the online medical abortion service Women on Web shipped abortion pills to 1,642 women in Ireland, and 5,600 women in Ireland tried to buy abortion pills from Women on Web in the five-year period January 2010 to December 2015: Aiken, Abigail et al, 'Experiences and Characteristics of Women Seeking and Completing At-home Medical Termination of Pregnancy through Online Telemedicine in Ireland and Northern Ireland: A Population-based Analysis' (2017) 124(8) *British Journal of Obstetrics & Gynaecology* 1208.

[38] Section 8, Information (Services outside the State for Termination of Pregnancy) Act 1995. See further the discussion in Chapter 4.

The 8th Amendment: beyond abortion

While repeal of the 8th Amendment is most often discussed in the context of abortion—and that is the primary focus of this book—its reach, and thus the arguments for reform, go well beyond that. The Amendment refers to the 'life' of the 'unborn' in general, rather than to abortion in particular, so that the whole duration of pregnancy, including labour and birth, comes within its scope. When a voluntarily pregnant person becomes ill, and needs an abortion, the 8th Amendment applies. It is less clear whether the law requires that treatment for a serious illness, such as cancer, should be delayed or denied if it would have severe consequences for the foetus.[39] We do know, however, that an otherwise healthy pregnant person may be subjected to unwanted medical treatment under the 8th Amendment. Ordinarily, adults are entitled to refuse consent to any medical intervention for any reason.[40] However, the Health Service Executive's (HSE) National Consent Policy departs from this position where pregnant people are concerned. It states that under the 8th Amendment:

> the consent of a pregnant woman is required for all health and social care interventions. However ... there is significant legal uncertainty regarding the pregnant woman's right to refuse

[39] See further Lalor, Joan et al, *Report on a Multidisciplinary Analysis of the Protection of Life During Pregnancy Act* (2015, TARA), available at www.tara.tcd.ie/handle/2262/80584. See discussion to this effect in *Attorney General v X* (see note 6).

[40] See *Re a Ward of Court (withholding medical treatment) (No 2)* [1996] 2 IR 79; *JM v Board of Management of St Vincent's Hospital* [2003] 1 IR 321. That right would also, of course, include the right to refuse consent to abortion: *SPUC v Grogan* [1989] IR 753, 767. In the UK, the courts will not entertain an application to overrule a woman's refusal of Caesarean section unless her mental capacity is in issue. See, for example, *St George's Healthcare NHS Trust v S* [1998] 3 All ER 673; *Re MB* [1997] 38 BMLR 175 CA; *Montgomery v Lanarkshire Health Board (General Medical Council intervening)* [2015] UKSC 11.

treatment in circumstances in which the refusal would place the life of a viable foetus at serious risk. In such circumstances, legal advice should be sought as to whether an application to the High Court is necessary.[41]

This interpretation of the 8th Amendment constructs the pregnant person and her foetus as adversaries, even where she does not intend to terminate the pregnancy, but wishes to make a decision (for example, attempting vaginal birth instead of Caesarean section) that her medical team considers too risky. The new National Maternity Strategy goes even further, stating that a pregnant person's decision making in pregnancy should be respected only 'insofar as it is safe to do so', and that her decision may be overridden, not only where there are implications for the 'life of the baby', but for its health 'as defined by her team of health care professionals'.[42] The Association of Maternity Services Ireland (AIMSI)[43] and Midwives for Choice[44]

---

[41] Health Service Executive, *National Consent Policy* (2014, revised May 2016). For High Court cases, see *South Western Health Board v K and Anor* [2002] IEHC 104; *Health Service Executive v F* (High Court, *ex tempore*, Birmingham J., 20 November 2010); *Mother A v Waterford Regional Hospital* (High Court, Hedigan J., 11 March 2013). Difficulties may also arise over advance directives, if a pregnant person loses her decision-making capacity. See Association for Improvements in Maternity Services – Ireland, *Submission to the Citizens' Assembly on the Eighth Amendment to the Constitution* (2016), pp 17-19, available at http://aimsireland.ie/wp-content/uploads/2016/12/AIMSI-Submission-CitizensAssemblyArt40.3.3-FINAL-1.pdf.

[42] Department of Health, *Creating a Better Future Together: National Maternity Strategy 2016-2026* (2016). See Egan, Emily, 'The Role of Article 40.3.3 in Medical and Parental Decision-Making', presentation to the Citizens' Assembly, 4 March 2017.

[43] Association for Improvements in Maternity Services – Ireland, 'What Matters To You Survey 2014' (2014), available at http://aimsireland.ie/what-matters-to-you-survey-2015/womens-experiences-of-consent-in-the-irish-maternity-services.

[44] Midwives for Choice, *Submission to the United Nations Committee Against Torture (CAT) for Ireland's Second Periodic Examination under*

report that women have been threatened with arrest or court action where they would not comply with their medical teams' requirements.

In *HSE v B*,[45] the High Court clarified that pregnant people cannot be subjected to highly invasive surgery where the risks to the foetus from refusal are low. However, it is difficult to say with clarity how the Amendment affects pregnancy where the risks are higher, or the proposed treatment less obviously invasive. United Nations (UN) human rights bodies have criticised the use of coercive and medically unnecessary treatment in Irish labour wards[46] and AIMSI reports that women are routinely coerced to accede to tests, procedures and medical treatment in Irish maternity care.[47] Pregnant people's refusal of medical treatment has been overridden by the courts; for example, in Ms Y's case, the High Court granted orders for forcible feeding and hydration in order to maintain a woman's pregnancy against her will, and would have permitted a Caesarean section without her consent, even though her decision-making capacity was not in question.[48] The courts are already aware of how oppressive coerced medical treatment can be. In *HSE v B*,[49] Twomey J. held that the performance of a Caesarean section on a pregnant woman against her will, with the necessary force

---

the *Convention Against Torture and Other Cruel, Inhuman or Degrading Treatment or Punishment* (2017), p 5, available at http://midwivesforchoice. ie/wp-content/uploads/2017/01/MfC-Submission-to-UN-CAT.pdf.

[45] [2016] IEHC 605.

[46] United Nations Committee on the Elimination of Discrimination against Women (UNCEDAW), *Concluding Observations on the Combined Sixth and Seventh Periodic Reports of Ireland*, CEDAW/C/IRL/CO/6-7, 9 March 2017; United Nations Committee Against Torture (UNCAT), *Concluding Observations on the Second Periodic Report of Ireland*, CAT/C/IRL/CO/2, 31 August 2017.

[47] Association for Improvements in Maternity Services – Ireland (2014) (see note 43). See further http://midwivesforchoice.ie/wp-content/ uploads/2017/01/MfC-Submission-to-UN-CAT.pdf, pp 8-9.

[48] See further Fletcher, Ruth, 'Contesting the Cruel Treatment of Abortion-Seeking Women' (2014) 22(44) *Reproductive Health Matters* 10.

[49] *HSE v B* [2016] IEHC 605.

and restraint that such a procedure entails, would be a 'grievous assault' and 'a gross violation of her right to bodily integrity'.[50]

We cannot simply assert that this system is ultimately safe for pregnant people. Reproductive rights campaigners point out that we do not accurately record all cases in which pregnant people have suffered long-term health consequences as a result of their pregnancy.[51] We only record deaths and 'near misses'.[52]

Even where no dispute arises around consent, the 8th Amendment is a crucial part of a long-established Irish medico-legal culture that diminishes, disempowers and has potential to harm pregnant people. It is troubling that non-consensual treatment of pregnant people continues in Ireland even as we seek to redress the historical injustice of symphysiotomy.[53] Repeal of the 8th Amendment would represent a commitment to ensuring that past institutional violations of women's rights do not recur. It would also reflect a shift in our societal understanding of where the burdens of motherhood should begin and end. While an individual might decide to take on the risk of ill health or trauma as the cost of birthing a baby, increasingly Irish voters understand that the Constitution should not *compel* a person to do so.

---

[50] *HSE v B* [2016] IEHC 605, [16].

[51] In 2015, the severe maternal morbidity rate was 6.35 per 1,000: Manning, Edel et al, *Severe Maternal Morbidity in Ireland: Annual Report 2014* (2017, National Perinatal Epidemiology Centre), p 8. See also the MAMMI study, which takes a more expansive approach to morbidity, but studies only a fraction of first-time mothers, available at www.mammi.ie/surveys.php.

[52] See further Murphy-Lawless, Jo, 'Embodied Truths: Women's Struggle for Voice and Wellbeing in Irish Maternity Services', in Quilty, Aideen et al (eds) *The Abortion Papers Ireland: Volume 2* (2015, Cork University Press). If passed, the Coroners' Amendment Bill (2017) would ensure mandatory inquests in cases of maternal death.

[53] See further Enright, Máiréad, 'Ireland, Symphysiotomy and UNHRC', Inherently Human, 21 July 2014, available at https://inherentlyhuman. wordpress.com/2014/07/21/ireland-symphysiotomy-and-the-unhrc.

Towards repeal: what has happened?

In all likelihood, there will be a referendum on the 8th Amendment in 2018. The story of how we got to this point is beyond the scope of a book of this length. Collective and individual activism over decades, feminist solidarity and enablement of women in seeking and accessing abortion care, individual instances of people speaking out about their experiences, rallies and marches, and personal conversations about the 8th Amendment are all part of the social mobilisation—led by women—to demand a change to the Constitution. So too are stories of the harm caused to pregnant people by the 8th Amendment and the oppressive cultures that it reflects, creates and perpetuates: Sheila Hodgers, who died in 1983 after being denied treatment for cancer because it might harm her unborn child; 'X', who in 1992, was temporarily prevented from travelling to end a pregnancy resulting from rape and who, we assume, has had to endure a political system that persistently discusses her traumatic teenage experience for the past 25 years and more;[54] Savita Halappanavar, who in 2012 died of sepsis during a prolonged miscarriage in a hospital in Galway;[55] Michelle Harte, who accessed abortion in the UK having been denied both cancer treatment and an abortion, in spite of medical advice to terminate the pregnancy;[56] 'Ms Y', who, although suicidal, could not access abortion and instead was subjected to an early Caesarean section to secure early delivery;[57] the thousands of women who have scrimped, saved, begged and borrowed to travel abroad to end their pregnancies; the thousands more who have been unable to do so.

Although most political parties campaigning in the 2016 General Election recognised that the 8th Amendment was an issue,[58] there

---

[54] *Attorney General v X* (see note 6).

[55] See HSE, *Report of Incident 50278* (2013), pp 5-6.

[56] Cullen, Paul, 'State Settled with Cancer Patient', *The Irish Times*, 22 November 2012.

[57] See Fletcher, Ruth (note 48).

[58] Fine Gael Election Manifesto 2016, pp 71-72; Sinn Fein General Election Manifesto 2016, p 45; Labour Party General Election Manifesto 2016, p

was no consensus on reform. The Programme for Partnership Government agreed in the spring of 2016 included a commitment to establish a Citizens' Assembly to discuss the 8th Amendment (among other things).[59] That Assembly began to operate in autumn 2016 and reported to the Oireachtas in June of 2017.[60] We consider its recommendations throughout this book, but the primary point for now is that, following months of evidence, testimony, submissions, deliberations, and legal and medical advice, the Assembly reached the view that the constitutional status quo could not be sustained.[61] Eighty-seven per cent of the Assembly agreed that Article 40.3.3 'should not be retained in full'. On 18 October 2017, the Joint Oireachtas Committee established to consider whether and how to give effect to the Assembly's recommendations passed a similar proposal: that the Amendment should not be retained in full.

The issue that then arises is how to give legal effect to these decisions. How can, and should, the Constitution be changed? What kind of legislation should be introduced to secure access to abortion? And what principles should underpin new law? This book is intended for anyone, lawyer or not, activist or not, who is interested in answering those questions.

7; Anti-Austerity Alliance General Election Manifest 2016, p 3; People Before Profit General Election Manifesto 2016, pp 18-19; Social Democrats General Election Manifesto 2016, p 39; Green Party General Election Manifesto 2016, p 52. Fianna Fail was an exception: there is no mention of the 8th Amendment in *An Ireland for All: Manifesto 2016*. However, following a number of changes of mind, the party leader proposed a judge-led commission to consider the 8th Amendment: Newstalk radio interview with Micheál Martin TD, 2 December 2015.

[59] Department of the Taoiseach, *A Programme for Partnership Government* (2016), p 153.

[60] The Citizens' Assembly, *First Report and Recommendations of the Citizens' Assembly: The Eighth Amendment of the Constitution* (2017).

[61] For a critical account of the Assembly proceedings, see Enright, Máiréad, '#Strike4Repeal: Ireland's Women's Strike', Critical Legal Thinking, 8 March 2017, available at http://criticallegalthinking.com/2017/03/08/strike4repeal-irelands-womens-strike.

2

The Constitution after the 8th

As we saw in Chapter 1, the 8th Amendment was and is a deliberate and extraordinary attempt to defend a conservative idea of the Constitution against the anticipated effects of social change. It was inserted to prevent the ordinary development of constitutional rights, specifically reproductive rights, within a 'living' constitutional text. Over time, this rot has taken hold at all levels of the constitutional law on abortion, producing a body of abortion law that is obstinately resistant to change. The stability of this constitutional order has meant the steady oppression of pregnant people. It is crucial that, in reforming that law, we abandon the damaging urge to seek 'legal certainty', essentially inherited from the Pro-Life Amendment Campaign, and reopen abortion law to our ordinary, if flawed, processes of constitutional interpretation. In this chapter, we set out an agenda for how that might be achieved.

Options for constitutional reform

The Joint Oireachtas Committee on the Eighth Amendment was established to consider the recommendations of the Citizens' Assembly, and to advise the Oireachtas on constitutional and legislative abortion law reform. Like the Assembly, the Committee accepts that constitutional space must be made to liberalise abortion law. The only way to do that is through a referendum,[1] and voters must be presented with a simple proposition to which they can vote 'yes' or 'no'.[2] The Committee has considered six options for constitutional reform. These are as follows:

1. Simple repeal of the 8th Amendment.
2. Simple repeal of the 8th Amendment, and publication of draft or outline legislation liberalising abortion access before the referendum. This legislation could not be passed until the 8th Amendment was repealed.
3. Replacing the 8th Amendment with a new constitutional provision setting out 'grounds' for abortion access (defined sets of circumstances in which a pregnant person would be entitled to access an abortion).
4. Replacing the 8th Amendment with a provision entrenching new abortion legislation in the Constitution. The legislation, presumably, would set out new, more liberal, grounds for abortion access than are currently contained in the Protection of Life During Pregnancy Act 2013 (PLDPA).[3]
5. Replacing the 8th Amendment with a provision setting out a new balance of constitutional rights as between the pregnant person and the foetus she is carrying (or amending the 8th to the same effect).[4]

---

[1] Article 46.2, Constitution of Ireland.

[2] The Constitution Review Group was of the view that a 'preferendum' (in which voters would indicate preferences between a range of options for constitutional reform) was not possible under the Constitution: The All-Party Oireachtas Committee on the Constitution, *Report of the Constitution Review Group 1996* (1996), Item 7 considered in respect of Articles 46 and 47.

[3] This was attempted in the 2002 abortion referendum; *Morris and Ní Mhaoldomnaigh v Minister for Environment* (unreported, High Court, 1 February 1 2002).

[4] See, for example, Gerard Whyte's proposal that the 8th Amendment be retained in substance, but the word 'equal' removed, as reported in McGarry, Patsy 'Repealing Eighth "Removes Constitutional Protection for Unborn"', *The Irish Times*, 20 October 2017.

6. A provision providing that the Oireachtas shall have the exclusive power to decide on the content of abortion legislation, and that this legislation shall not be subject to review by the courts.[5]

We argue that simple repeal of the 8th Amendment (option 1), whether or not legislation is published before the referendum (option 2), is the most sensible of these proposals. Option 2 could provide voters with a concrete indication of the legislation that would follow repeal, and thus help to inform the referendum campaign. However, the legislation actually passed might differ (in big or small ways) from the outline published before the referendum. In Chapters 3 and 4, we outline the shape that any such legislation should take.

Options 3-6, however, are potentially very cumbersome: they are difficult to design and use, and might generate confusing and distracting debate during a referendum campaign. More importantly, they are, in our view, misguided attempts to address particular kinds of 'legal uncertainty' perceived to arise from simple repeal. The basic idea behind this invocation of 'legal uncertainty' is that, if the 8th Amendment is removed, the constitutional bedrock of our abortion law is gone. According to this position, after repeal we would move from an old legal position in which the limits of abortion law, however narrow and punitive, are perceived to be clearly defined into a new one in which they seem to be much less clear. For people who take this position, the key question seems to be 'What would replace the 8th?'[6] Without a specific constitutional provision on abortion, we would need to decide what the remainder of the Constitution

---

[5] It would be possible to provide explicitly for the Oireachtas to make law on abortion without immunising the legislation from constitutional review. However, that does not seem to be the Committee's understanding. See Fiona de Londras, Opening Statement, evidence to Joint Committee on the Eighth Amendment to the Constitution, 27 September 2017 and the discussion of the Committee on options for constitutional change on 18 October 2017.

[6] The former Taoiseach, Enda Kenny, for example, said that he would not contemplate repeal of the 8th Amendment without knowing what might replace it: Newstalk radio interview, 11 September 2015.

'says' about how abortion should be regulated. To be more precise, we would need to wait and see what the institutions empowered to interpret the Constitution—the Oireachtas and the courts—decide on what the remainder of the Constitution 'says' about how abortion should be regulated. There are two apparent concerns here. First, if the electorate voted to repeal the 8th Amendment, the Oireachtas might pass new abortion legislation that is more or less liberal than some voters are willing to accept. Second, if the electorate voted to repeal the 8th Amendment, the courts might strike down new abortion legislation because it is too liberal, or too conservative, to meet the demands of the altered constitutional text.[7] Repeal of the 8th Amendment *seems* to introduce a new measure of unpredictability into Irish abortion law. While we accept that these uncertainties may be sources of political concern, they are really very ordinary features of our constitutional system.

Everyday constitutional interpretation

The current debate about constitutional abortion law reform is, in some senses, a debate about text. Constitutions are written in broad, open-textured language. Every part of the constitutional text is capable of holding many meanings; reasonable people, and reasonable lawyers, may disagree about how text is to be interpreted.[8] In interpreting a constitution, we do not have to remain within the 'four corners' of the document. Rather, we read the document in its societal context. So, established or accepted meanings of a constitutional right might

---

[7] This power is set out in Article 15.4, Constitution of Ireland.

[8] A good example might be the constitutional text on marriage. Before 2015, some people thought that the right to marry under the Constitution could apply to same-sex and opposite-sex couples. Others thought that the constitutional text would require an amendment to achieve this. The latter point of view won out, in the courts and in the Oireachtas, so that it was necessary to hold the marriage equality referendum: *Zappone & Gilligan v Revenue Commissioners & Ors* [2006] 2 IR 417; 34th Amendment to the Constitution Act 1935.

evolve over time, as society changes. The Constitution is a living document.[9] It cannot be 'certain', if by 'certain' we mean 'having only one meaning for all time'. So, for example, even if we repealed the 8th Amendment, we would not return to the constitutional abortion law as it was in 1982. The remainder of the Constitution would be interpreted taking into account relevant legal and social changes that have happened since then. The text has not remained static.

Understanding the unfixed or 'indeterminate' nature of constitutional provisions affects how we understand the role of text in the reform of our constitutional abortion law. Whatever change is made to the text of the Constitution through a referendum, we can only *predict* how it will be read in practice; we cannot tell for certain. That is true whether we repeal or replace the 8th Amendment. If, as discussed in the next section, we were to vote to insert new words into the Constitution according to Options 3, 4 or 5, those words might in the future be held to have a meaning that many of us did not expect or anticipate. We can also say, of course, that we can make good educated guesses about how even new constitutional arrangements could be interpreted, based on previous case law and patterns of interpretation. In Chapter 3, we do just that.

Under our constitutional system, we rely (sometimes gratefully and sometimes reluctantly) on state institutions to produce authoritative and reasonably settled interpretations of the constitutional text. In judicial terms, the Supreme Court, in particular, is the final decision maker on matters of constitutional interpretation.[10] It interprets the Constitution in judgments responding to cases brought by individual litigants. We rely on it (and the Constitution empowers it)[11] to decide, using established specialist techniques of legal interpretation, which of the possible meanings attributable to a section of constitutional text is most plausible and most authoritative. Often, aspects of the interpretation of a particular constitutional provision remain unclear

---

[9] *Per* Walsh J. in *McGee v Attorney General* [1974] IR 284.

[10] Article 34.3.2, Article 34.5, Constitution of Ireland.

[11] Articles 34-37, Constitution of Ireland.

for years; for example, we discuss some unsettled aspects of the 8th Amendment in the next section. However, we generally expect that, over time, and with repeated cases, certain interpretations of constitutional provisions will become settled.

In focusing on the judiciary, however, we often forget the Oireachtas' fundamental role in interpreting the Constitution. Ordinarily, when the Oireachtas is considering new legislation, it decides for itself what restrictions the Constitution places on its actions and builds new legislation accordingly. The Attorney General, in particular, will advise the Government—which subsequently advises the Oireachtas—about whether a legislative proposal is vulnerable to later challenge in the courts.[12] Usually, these processes provide enough certainty for law-making purposes. In addition, as a matter of law, legislation enjoys a 'presumption of constitutionality',[13] and if nobody ever challenges it successfully in the courts, it remains securely in place, for good or ill. The courts generally assume that when the Oireachtas makes a law it respects its obligation to do so in a constitutionally compatible way.[14] Courts will be especially deferential to the Oireachtas' decisions where it has legislated on an issue considered to be morally controversial.[15] It is rare for legislation to be struck down as unconstitutional. Thus, the courts' powers to interpret the Constitution have not usually impeded the work of the Oireachtas. Even on controversial issues, the legal order generally remains stable. If the Supreme Court interprets the Constitution in a way that the majority of people consider inappropriate, the Oireachtas can (and often does) offer voters the opportunity to reverse that interpretation by a 'corrective referendum'.[16]

---

[12] Article 30.1, Constitution of Ireland.

[13] *People (AG) v O'Callaghan* [1966] 1 IR 501; *East Donegal Co-op Ltd v Attorney General* [1970] 1 IR 317.

[14] Article 15.4, Constitution of Ireland.

[15] See generally Foley, Brian, *Deference and the Presumption of Constitutionality* (2008, IPA).

[16] On 'corrective' referenda, see de Londras, Fiona, and Gwynn Morgan, David, 'Constitutional Amendment in Ireland', in Contiades, Xenephon (ed)

Abortion law as an exception to everyday constitutional interpretation

If we return to the six options for constitutional reform considered by the Joint Committee, we see that many of them are designed to intervene in this ordinary process of constitutional interpretation. Some are mechanical interventions, designed to guarantee 'legal certainty' by placing certain interpretations of the Constitution, and associated legislation, beyond bounds. Others are attempts to 'constitutionalise' abortion law; they aim to secure 'legal certainty' by continuing to regulate abortion in some detail in the constitutional text rather than in legislation alone.

Mechanical interventions

Options 2-5 are attempts to constrain the Oireachtas' ordinary power to pass new abortion legislation after removal of the 8th Amendment. Although their content has not been spelled out, in principle, they could be read as attempts to ensure 'legal certainty' by setting firm boundaries to future abortion legislation. Option 2 is the least restrictive, since the Oireachtas cannot be compelled to pass any particular legislation, although political pressure might have that effect in practice. Options 3 and 5 are more restrictive still, since, depending on their content, they could prevent the Oireachtas from passing legislation providing for more extensive abortion access than was set out in the Constitution. Option 3 is more directive than option 5; it would set out specific grounds for accessing abortion, rather than broad principles for abortion regulation. Option 4 seems to bind the Oireachtas most tightly, since it would enshrine detailed abortion legislation in the Constitution that could not be amended, even for minor reasons, without a referendum. Options 3 and 5, however, also ensure that, in at least some circumstances, a referendum would be required to change new abortion law. It goes without saying, of course,

Engineering Constitutional Change: A Comparative Perspective on Europe, Canada and the USA (2012, Routledge).

that it is more difficult to change abortion law in a referendum than to amend simple legislation.

Option 6 is directed, not at controlling the Oireachtas, but at controlling the judiciary.[17] It is a clear and very unusual effort to constrain the courts' ordinary power to strike down future abortion legislation as unconstitutional if necessary.[18] In principle, this provision could be read as protecting either liberal or conservative abortion legislation from undemocratic 'judicial activism'—interpretations of the Constitution that go beyond the presumed preferences of the majority of voters. However, option 6 would immunise future abortion legislation from judicial examination in almost all cases. This is potentially a very conservative step because it would make it difficult, if not impossible, for individuals to challenge abortion legislation in the courts regardless of the extent of its incursion into their constitutional rights.[19]

Although the 8th Amendment is different in shape from options 2–6, our experience of it should make us wary of any attempts to insulate abortion from the ordinary processes of constitutional interpretation. Constitutional development of Irish abortion law under the 8th Amendment long ago ground to a standstill. The Oireachtas has been unusually unwilling to assume that abortion legislation attracts the presumption of constitutionality or to propose legislation that runs even a minimal risk of unconstitutionality. Until the PLDPA, there

---

[17] As discussed further, options 3, 4 and 5 have significant impact on how a court would decide an abortion case after constitutional reform. For example, the judiciary would need to interpret the text of any constitutional amendments to decide what they mean in practice, and to determine whether any new abortion legislation is constitutional.

[18] David Kenny, evidence to the Joint Committee on the Eighth Amendment to the Constitution, 27 September 2017. The judiciary is only excluded in this way in a small number of areas of law, for example, emergency powers legislation when the state is at war.

[19] de Londras, Fiona, 'An Abortion Law Immune from Constitutional Review?', Human Rights in Ireland, 28 September 2017, available at http://humanrights.ie/constitution-of-ireland/an-abortion-law-immune-from-constitutional-review.

was no legislation explaining precisely when and how a woman could access abortion. The only abortion legislation in force for most of the life of the 8th Amendment—Offences against the Person Act 1861— criminalised abortion. For 20 years, doctors and pregnant people, and their legal advisers, had to interpret and apply for themselves the bare constitutional abortion law, as contained in the *X* case,[20] in the expectation that they were liable to imprisonment if they got it wrong. As Savita Halappanavar's case demonstrated,[21] this meant that abortion was inaccessible even in cases where it was arguably constitutional. Although the superior courts had asked the Oireachtas to pass abortion access legislation—to 'legislate for X'—on numerous occasions,[22] this did not happen until after the European Court of Human Rights in a case called *A, B and C v Ireland* found that the lack of legislation establishing a clear procedure for accessing lawful abortion was a breach of human rights.[23]

This near-complete 'chilling' of legislative agency is especially dangerous because, even if the judiciary is willing to soften the Amendment's edges, abortion can be particularly inaccessible to judicial innovation. Cases about the 8th Amendment have more often been brought at the instigation of the state, by service providers, or by anti-abortion campaigners, rather than by pregnant people themselves. People seeking abortion do not usually take cases to try to access abortion care unless they are restricted by their circumstances (for example, being in the care of the state). They have neither the resources nor the time, and they also are unlikely to want the

---

[20] *Attorney General v X* [1992] 1 IR 1.

[21] HSE, *Final Report: Investigation of Incident 50278* (2013), pp 5-6 and 71-73, identifying the law as a causal factor in relation to her death. See also Peter Boylan, evidence to the Joint Committee on the Eighth Amendment to the Constitution, 18 October 2017.

[22] See comments of McCarthy J. at 147 in *Attorney General v X* (see note 20); McCarthy J. in *SPUC v Grogan* [1989] IR 753, 770, and McKechnie J. in *D (A Minor) v Judge Brennan, the HSE, Ireland, and the Attorney General* (unreported, High Court, 9 May 2007).

[23] *A, B and C v Ireland* [2011] 53 EHRR 13.

publicity and distress that may come with litigation. In any event, the courts' restrictive interpretations of the 8th Amendment have likely discouraged litigants from bringing constitutional cases at all. Crucially, until recently, no government has considered the possibility of coming to pregnant people's aid, by taking up its ordinary responsibility to develop the Constitution by offering a referendum to liberalise Irish abortion law. We are not arguing that these roadblocks to constitutional interpretation were the *necessary* result of the 8th Amendment; rather, they have their roots in a variety of political strategies developed over three decades, too numerous and complex to examine here. Our point is that it would be foolhardy to formalise these damaging political habits, and directly enshrine them in constitutional text.

Keeping abortion in the constitutional text

Some readers might argue that, if only we could select the perfect constitutional text to govern abortion, we might generate a new legal atmosphere in which the Oireachtas and the judiciary would be willing once more to develop constitutional abortion law within appropriate limits. They may be attracted to options 3, 4 and 5 for that reason. Options 3 and 4 suggest that the Constitution should effectively specify more or less detailed grounds for abortion access in the text. Option 5 preserves the idea, currently represented by the 8th Amendment, that the Constitution should contain a general express statement about how the rights of pregnant people should be limited or weighed against legal rights that we might bestow on the foetus. It is broader and more vague than Options 3 and 4, because it does not specify the circumstances in which abortion should be legally available. Contentious litigation would almost inevitably follow insertion of options 3–5 into the Constitution. In the meantime, past experience with the 8th Amendment suggests that the scope of the Oireachtas' law-making power would become unclear, leaving medics and their legal advisers to make clinical decisions in a situation that feels little changed from the status quo.

Advocates of options 3-5 are allying themselves with a model of constitutional abortion law that has very few comparators elsewhere in the world. Most countries do not try to make abortion law in the constitution. A handful of states provide the explicit constitutional protection of foetal rights suggested in option 5. However, only Ireland and the Philippines confer 'equal' protection on pregnant people and foetuses.[24] Other countries provide for a broader protection of foetal life. In Chile, the provision is somewhat more prosaic—'The law protects the life of the unborn'[25]—while the Andorran Constitution says that the right to life is 'fully protect[ed] in its different phases'.[26] The constitutions of Peru and Honduras say that 'the unborn' is considered to have rights as if it were born.[27] In all of these states, access to abortion is extremely limited, and in some states was absolutely prohibited at one stage even when the life of the pregnant woman was in danger.

Some other states approach abortion in their constitutions not by asserting prenatal rights, but by explicitly outlining the power of the parliament to pass legislation relating to abortion. In Zambia,[28] Zimbabwe,[29] Uganda,[30] Kenya[31] and Swaziland,[32] abortion is unlawful unless, and to the extent only, that is provided for by law. In a few countries, the constitution actually specifies when abortion is permitted by law, as suggested in options 3 and 4 above. Kenya's Constitution provides that abortion can be made available in cases of emergency and risk to life or health, as well as other situations provided

---

[24] Section 12, Constitution of the Philippines 1987.

[25] Article 19(1), Constitution of Chile 1980 with amendments through 2015.

[26] Article 8(1), Constitution of the Principality of Andorra 1993.

[27] Article 67, Constitution of the Republic of Honduras 1982; Article 2(1), Constitution of Peru 1993 with amendments through 2009.

[28] Article 12(2), Constitution of Zambia 1991 with amendments through 2009.

[29] Article 48(3), Constitution of Zimbabwe 2013.

[30] Article 22(2), Constitution of Uganda 1995 with amendments through 2005.

[31] Article 26(4), Constitution of Kenya 2010.

[32] Article 5, The Constitution of Swaziland 2005.

for by law.[33] The Somalian Constitution limits abortion availability to cases of necessity, especially to save the life of the mother.[34] Swaziland's Constitution provides that abortion may be allowed on medical or therapeutic grounds,[35] including cases where a doctor certifies that continued pregnancy will endanger the life or constitute a serious threat to the physical or mental health of the woman, where there is serious risk that the child will suffer from a 'physical or mental defect of such a nature that the child will be irreparably seriously handicapped',[36] where the pregnancy resulted from rape, incest or 'unlawful sexual intercourse with a mentally retarded female',[37] or in other situations provided for by law.[38] In both Kenya and Swaziland, however, abortion is actually inaccessible in practice: there is no legislation to regulate it, illegal and unsafe abortion is a major public health problem, and there are no indications that abortion will actually be legalised.[39] Globally, constitutional structures akin to options 3–5 are not associated with good public health outcomes.[40]

Proponents of options 3–5 may argue, nevertheless, that we can only ensure 'legal certainty' in the regulation of abortion by expressly regulating abortion in the Constitution. As we have discussed, the meaning of any constitutional provision falls to be determined by courts; the pursuit of absolute certainty through drafting is futile.[41]

---

[33] Article 26(4), Constitution of Kenya 2010.

[34] Article 15(5), Constitution of Somalia 2012.

[35] Article 5(a), Constitution of Swaziland 2005.

[36] Article 5(a)(i-iii), Constitution of Swaziland 2005.

[37] Article 5(b), Constitution of Swaziland 2005.

[38] Article 5(c), Constitution of Swaziland 2005.

[39] For Kenya, see in general Center for Reproductive Rights, *In Harm's Way: The Impact of Kenya's Restrictive Abortion Law* (2010).

[40] See further Enright, Máiréad, 'Why Would Any Country Put Abortion in the Constitution?', Human Rights in Ireland, 20 April 2017, available at http://humanrights.ie/constitution-of-ireland/why-would-a-country-put-abortion-in-the-constitution.

[41] Fiona de Londras, evidence to the Joint Committee on the Eighth Amendment to the Constitution, 27 September 2017; Ms Justice Mary Laffoy, evidence to the Joint Committee on the Eighth Amendment to the Constitution, 20

This position is borne out by our experience of the 8th Amendment. Whether the language of text intended to replace the 8th is broad, as in option 5, or narrow as in options 3 and 4, it will depend on interpretation for its meaning. Interpretation may be more expansive, or more rigid, than anticipated. In Chapter 1, we discussed how quickly the interpretation of the 8th Amendment ossified, providing only limited relief to pregnant people who required abortions. More importantly, even 35 years after its insertion into the Constitution, the 8th Amendment has not conferred complete 'certainty' on our abortion law. Many of those who supported its introduction, for example, were surprised to see it used to establish a limited right to abortion in case of risk to life from suicide in the X case.[42] Others were surprised to see it used in childbirth cases where no abortion was sought,[43] or in immigration cases.[44] Even at its very core, the 8th Amendment has been unable to clothe the 'unborn' in 'legal certainty'. There are at least three issues here, which we discuss in turn.

Defining the unborn

First, although the PLDPA defines unborn life for the purposes of that Act,[45] there is no general authoritative definition of 'the unborn' under the 8th Amendment. In all likelihood, it refers to an 'embryo post implantation',[46] but it has not been considered in any case about abortion access under the 8th Amendment.

September 2017; David Kenny, evidence to the Joint Committee on the Eighth Amendment to the Constitution, 27 September 2017.

[42] *Attorney General v X* (see note 20).

[43] *Health Service Executive v B* [2016] IEHC 605.

[44] *Baby O v MJELR* [2002] IR169.

[45] Section 1 defines 'unborn' as 'human life ... during the period of time commencing after implantation in the womb of a woman and ending on the complete emergence of the life from the body of the woman'.

[46] *Roche v Roche* [2009] IESC 82.

Foetal rights

Second, we do not know whether the foetus *only* has a right to life under the Constitution, or whether it has a broader range of constitutional rights. Although the constitutional right to life of the foetus was expressly introduced by the 8th Amendment, some judges claimed that it existed prior to this, as an unenumerated constitutional right.[47] (An unenumerated right is an implicit constitutional right. Although not written into the Constitution, unenumerated rights are still protected by it, and the courts identify them and set their scope.) Questions about the extent of foetal rights were not materially important to the decisions made in these cases, meaning that these comments were *obiter* (that is, not binding interpretations). However, they suggest that there might be a whole set of foetal rights that existed before, and might continue to exist after, the 8th Amendment.[48] Second, there are conflicting decisions from the High Court on whether the right to life is the only prenatal constitutional right in Ireland, or whether the foetus might have a larger set of constitutional rights, although these are not cases about access to abortion.[49]

---

[47] *Attorney General (SPUC) v Open Door Counselling Limited and the Wellwoman Centre Ltd* [1988] 1 IR 593; *Norris v Attorney General* [1984] IR 36; *Finn v Attorney General* [1983] IR 154; *McGee v Attorney General* [1974] IR 284; *G v An Bord Uchtala* [1980] IR 32.

[48] See further Enright, Máiréad et al, 'Abortion Law in Ireland: A Model for Change' (2015) 5(1) *feminists@law*.

[49] *Ugbelese v MJELR* [2009] IEHC 598; *E v MJELR* [2008] IEHC 68 (cited with approval by MacEochaidh J. in *FO v Minister for Justice* [2013] IEHC 236 and again in *Dos Santos v Minister for Justice* [2013] IEHC 237); *IRM v Minister for Justice, Equality and Law Reform* [2016] IEHC 478. See further Enright, Máiréad, 'The Rights of the Unborn: A Troubling Decision from the High Court', Human Rights in Ireland, 10 August 2016, available at http://humanrights.ie/uncategorized/the-rights-of-the-unborn-a-troubling-decision-from-the-high-court.

Fatal foetal abnormality

Third, we do not know whether the 8th Amendment permits abortion in cases of fatal foetal abnormality. Successive governments have taken the view that it would be unconstitutional to allow for abortion in such cases,[50] but there are good arguments to the contrary. On the one hand, the state need not take impracticable or futile steps to preserve foetal life, which suggests that the state may not prevent the termination of a pregnancy where the foetus has no prospect of life outside the womb. On the other hand, it is possible that the 8th does not permit abortion in such cases because the foetal abnormality does not by itself create a real and substantial risk to the life of the pregnant woman. Furthermore, since the 8th Amendment says nothing about the health of the foetus, it may be that in cases where there is any prospect, however small, that the foetus will be born alive, it is still 'unborn' and protected by the 8th Amendment.[51] In the absence of a Supreme Court decision on this precise issue, we simply do not know whether the 8th Amendment permits these pregnancies to be terminated. The Amendment has not even been able to provide the minimum degree of legal certainty to provide relief to some pregnant people affected by these diagnoses.

Repeal: legal certainty in its proper place

Those opposed to repeal of the 8th Amendment tend to argue that it would plunge the constitutional law on abortion into deep and unprecedented uncertainty. For example, some commentators have

---

[50] See unsuccessful Bills to permit abortion in cases of fatal foetal abnormality: Protection of Life During Pregnancy Act (Amendment) 2013 (Bill No. 115/2013); Protection of Life During Pregnancy Act (Amendment) 2015 (Bill No. 20/2015).

[51] *Attorney General v X* (see note 20); *PP v Health Service Executive* [2014] IEHC 622. See further Barrington, Eileen, 'Article 40.3.3 of the Constitution and Fatal Foetal Abnormality', presentation to the Citizens' Assembly, 7 January 2017.

suggested that repeal would generate uncertainty around the scope of the rights of the unborn, and that these might re-emerge to restrict future abortion legislation through judicial interpretation of the Constitution.[52] However, even if we think that these individual arguments are plausible, they overstate the degree of 'legal certainty' achievable within constitutional text: even the 8th Amendment has its chinks and gaps. We do not argue, of course, that simple repeal addresses these kinds of concerns with 'legal certainty'. As we discuss in Chapter 3, repeal of the 8th Amendment leaves the constitutionality of abortion to be determined by a clutch of constitutional rights most of which have never been applied to an abortion case before and will require development.

Our point is that this 'legal uncertainty' is not the unusual threat it has been represented to be. Moreover, as our review of options 2-6 demonstrates, the costs of seeking exceptional certainty through ever more elaborate constitutional texts may be much greater than its benefits. Repeal is not a risk-free proposition, but we need to become comfortable, again, with an ordinary level of constitutional (un)certainty around abortion. Rather than seek out complex

---

[52] Madden, Deirdre, *Medicine, Law and Ethics* (3rd edn) (2016, Bloomsbury Professional), pp 484-486; Wade, Katherine, 'Refusal of Emergency Caesarean Section in Ireland: A Relational Approach' (2014) 22(1) *Medical Law Review* 1; Fiona de Londras, written submission to the Citizens' Assembly (2016). Most commentators accept that the likelihood of unenumerated foetal rights being revived after repeal of the 8th Amendment is poor; Brian Murray, presentation to the Citizens' Assembly, 'Legal Consequences of Retention, Repeal, or Amendment of Article 40.3.3 of the Constitution' 14 March 2017; Fiona de Londras (see note 5). Although we do not recommend that any text should replace the 8th Amendment, we recognise that some people are concerned that, after repeal of the 8th, foetal rights could be developed by a conservative judiciary in ways that undermine access to abortion. This concern could be addressed by a minimalist replacement text intended to prevent any such interpretation. Such a provision could put the implicit meaning of repeal into words, providing that 'Nothing in this Constitution prohibits abortion as provided for by law', as proposed by Fiona de Londras (see note 5).

constitutional mechanisms to stave off 'legal uncertainty', lawmakers should adopt new principles for constitutional change, which put 'certainty' in its proper place.

Conclusion

In Chapter 3, we discuss how pregnant people's rights could be developed after repeal of the 8th Amendment. Consistent with this focus on the rights of pregnant people, we argue that it is appropriate to reconceive legal certainty for a post-repeal landscape. Political concern to secure exceptional kinds of 'legal certainty' suggests that abortion is an exceptional practice, that women's bodies are uniquely chaotic, unpredictable and perhaps disobedient. However, as we argue in Chapter 3, a rights-based approach to abortion requires us to accept that the pregnant person is best placed to make her own abortion decisions, and to normalise abortion as a medical treatment. A new conception of legal certainty would affirm secure rights to access abortion and other medical treatment in pregnancy, using transparent, predictable processes that support autonomous decision making. The Oireachtas could achieve such certainty by legislating appropriately, by providing timely guidance and training on how that legislation should be implemented, and by ensuring that pregnant people have access to accurate, non-directive, and non-judgmental information. In other words, such legal certainty is achieved through a mixture of measures: constitutional, legislative and regulatory.

Constitutional reform should also clearly empower the Oireachtas to respond quickly to scientific advances, public health crises and abuses of human rights. This means ensuring that the Oireachtas is free from unusual mechanical restraints of the kinds set out in options 2-6. The boundaries of the Oireachtas' legislative power should be set by respect for pregnant people's rights, and the Oireachtas should legislate in a way that attempts to vindicate those rights. Then, pregnant people who feel that legislators have misjudged the proper bounds of their rights are in a position to challenge the legislation in litigation, with a court ultimately deciding whose interpretation of the Constitution better serves the rights at stake. In other words, a reasonable level of legal certainty about abortion is the same as the level of certainty that the Oireachtas anticipates in all other areas of activity.

3

A rights-based approach to abortion

If the 8th Amendment were no longer part of our constitutional order, we would have the opportunity to redesign our approach to abortion law in Ireland. In this chapter, we address the possible shape and nature of a rights-based approach to abortion. Drawing on international human rights law, as well as on constitutional reproductive rights law in other countries, we consider the ways in which the constitutional rights ordinarily enjoyed by all persons in Ireland might be developed in the context of pregnancy. We also consider the state's powers to regulate abortion while respecting those rights.

Reimagining constitutional rights in pregnancy

Repealing the 8th Amendment would not automatically create an unlimited constitutional right to access abortion.[1] However, it

---

[1] For a discussion of this prospect, see Whyte, Gerard, 'Abortion on Demand the Legal Outcome of Repeal of the 8th Amendment', *The Irish Times,* 28 September 2016. See responses from Ivana Bacik and Fiona de Londras (*The Irish Times* letters page, 29 September 2016), the consequent rebuttal from Gerard Whyte (*The Irish Times* letters page, 30 September 2016) and further response from Fiona de Londras (*The Irish Times* letters page, 5 October 2016).

would generate opportunities to develop existing constitutional rights by recognising that the protection of constitutional rights requires access to lawful abortion in a range of circumstances. Since 1983, all questions about reproductive justice have been routed via the 8th Amendment and, therefore, folded into a concern with bare biological life; with keeping women and foetuses alive.[2] Under the 8th Amendment, once a woman becomes pregnant, the rights she can usually assert under the Constitution—to privacy, to bodily integrity, to equality—are subordinated to the right to life of the foetus. It is not that she no longer *holds* these rights, but that they are *weakened* by the foetus' right to life; she cannot assert a right to do anything that might endanger that life. In practice, this means that, at least in the context of abortion, those constitutional rights are held in abeyance: they have not been developed or interpreted by the courts in the context of pregnancy. If the 8th Amendment were no longer part of the Constitution, pregnant people's other rights might be reimagined for the Ireland that has emerged since 1983.[3]

---

[2] See Fletcher, Ruth, 'Judgment: *Attorney General v X*', in Enright, Máiréad et al (eds) *Northern/Irish Feminist Judgments: Judges' Troubles and the Gendered Politics of Identity* (2017, Hart/Bloomsbury Publishing). See also, for instance, *In Re Article 26 and the Regulation of Information (Services outside the State for Termination of Pregnancies) Bill 1995* [1995] IESC 9 rejecting an argument from the right to health as irrelevant. The suspension of pregnant people's constitutional rights, at least in an abortion context, was the explicit aim of the Pro-Life Action Campaign. See further McGuinness, Sheelagh, 'Commentary on *Attorney General v X*', in Enright, Máiréad et al (2017). For a counter-reading, suggesting that pregnant women's constitutional rights have received some consideration outside the abortion context, see Wade, Katherine, 'Caesarean Section Refusal in the Irish Courts: *Health Service Executive v B*' (2017) 35(3) *Medical Law Review* 494.

[3] When a substantial change is made to the constitutional text, that change should act as a nudge towards necessary interpretation, not only of the change itself (for example, to figure out the meaning of new text that is inserted) but also of its impact on the rest of the Constitution. As a general matter, the Constitution is interpreted 'harmoniously', so that the text is read as a coherent whole, and interpretations that reconcile apparently conflicting provisions with one another are preferred. It is thus to be expected

As discussed in Chapter 2, the Oireachtas is obliged to legislate within the bounds of the Constitution. This means that in making law, parliamentarians in Ireland are also involved in thinking about the requirements, limits and meaning of the Constitution.[4] We may also find that the courts have some role in interpreting the Constitution after the 8th Amendment, whether cases are brought by women seeking to liberalise abortion access, or by anti-abortion activists seeking to disrupt it.[5]

In mapping out possibilities for developing pregnant people's constitutional rights, we draw on international human rights law. We frequently hear that international human rights treaties have limited influence on Irish law.[6] It is important to be clear about the

---

that a change to the text might have broader implications for constitutional meaning. Where, as is the case with the 8th Amendment, one piece of text has dominated our constitutional understanding of how the law regulates a certain issue, the removal of that text will generate opportunities to figure out a new harmonious constitutional settlement about that issue; *Dillane v Ireland* [1980] ILRM 167.

[4] de Londras, Fiona, 'In Defence of Judicial Innovation and Constitutional Evolution', in Cahillane, Laura et al (eds) *Judges, Politics and the Irish Constitution* (2016, Manchester University Press).

[5] Although courts cannot ordinarily compel the Oireachtas to make new law, or direct fiscal and economic policy, they can strike an unconstitutional piece of law down, and order that the state remedy the harm that has been done through unconstitutional action, maybe by paying damages in some cases, and certainly by desisting from the activity at issue. As in any context, a case could take different forms: it might arise if the President were to refer a new abortion access bill to the Supreme Court to assess its constitutionality before signing it into law (under Article 26), or as a challenge from an individual pregnant person to the constitutionality of new abortion legislation, or it might be that questions of constitutional rights simply arise in the course of a case about the meaning and application of new abortion legislation in an unanticipated context.

[6] Coyne, Ellen, 'Abortion Law will be Decided by Voters, Varadkar tells UN', *The Times Ireland Edition*, (29 July 2017); Binchy, William, 'UN Committee's View on Abortion Contradicts Core Ethical Value of Human Rights', *The Irish Times*, 18 August 2014; Leahy, Pat, 'UN Abortion Ruling is "Not Binding", Enda Kenny says', *The Irish Times*, 15 June 2016.

difference between international and domestic law here. When Ireland ratifies a human rights treaty, it assumes a binding legal obligation in international law to ensure that the rights protected in that treaty are respected, protected and promoted in practice at home.[7] International courts and treaty bodies have some powers to enforce that obligation in the international sphere. In domestic law, human rights treaties are at their strongest when they have been explicitly incorporated into domestic law by the Oireachtas.[8] Incorporation of this kind is rare, and without it pregnant people cannot bring cases on the basis of international human rights in the Irish courts; they must bring those cases in international forums instead.[9] However, litigants may still rely on these rights when trying to *persuade* an Irish court that rights found in the Constitution should be interpreted to mirror international human rights principles.

As discussed in Chapter 2, the Constitution is a living document. Its meaning may develop over time to reflect the requirements of 'the common good', prudence, justice, charity, dignity, individual freedom and social order.[10] In deciding how these concepts help to define constitutional rights, Irish courts look at a wide range of sources,[11]

---

[7] Article 14, Vienna Convention on the Law of Treaties.

[8] Article 29.6, Constitution of Ireland. See, for example, *DF v Garda Commissioner* [2014] IEHC 213. On the status of the European Convention on Human Rights in Irish law, see *McD v L* [2010] IR 199; European Convention on Human Rights Act 2003; de Londras, Fiona, and Kelly, Clíona, *The European Convention on Human Rights Act: Operation, Impact and Analysis* (2010, Round Hall/Thompson Reuters).

[9] See, for example, *A, B and C v Ireland* [2011] 53 EHRR; *Mellet v Ireland*, Human Rights Committee, Communication no. 2324/2013 (2016); *Whelan v Ireland*, Human Rights Committee, Communication 2425/2014 (2017).

[10] Preamble, Constitution of Ireland 1937; *McGee v Attorney General* [1974] IR 284. For a recent example, see *NVH v MJELR* [2017] IESC 33, in which the Supreme Court found a right to work for asylum seekers, developing this from respect for the dignity of the person.

[11] See generally Hogan, Gerard, and Whyte, Gerard, *JM Kelly: The Irish Constitution* (4th edn) (2003, Bloomsbury Professional), chapter 1.

including international law.[12] This makes sense in the context of abortion law: the decisions of international human rights courts and monitoring bodies are a good guide to prevailing international norms on abortion regulation.[13] International human rights institutions also have extensive experience in articulating legal standards around abortion access, including in situations where there is deep division and disagreement about how access to abortion ought to be protected by international human rights law. Some of the approaches they have developed might be suitable for adoption in Ireland.[14] Furthermore, the current Irish abortion law violates numerous international human rights treaties.[15] If the 8th Amendment were repealed, Ireland's future compliance with international human rights law would be greatly helped if the courts articulated pregnant persons' rights in ways that reflect those protected under key international conventions.[16]

We are not arguing that the Irish courts should passively follow international human rights law when deciding the meaning of

---

[12] See, for example, *Attorney General v Damache* [2009] IESC 81; *People (DPP) v Gormley* [2014] IESC 17. For recent examples of constitutional courts elsewhere in the world that have taken account of international human rights law in developing abortion law, see Fine, Johanna et al, 'The Role of International Human Rights Norms in the Liberalization of Abortion Laws Globally' (2017) 19(1) *Health and Human Rights* 69.

[13] *People (DPP) v Gormley* (see note 12).

[14] On the usefulness of international and comparative law in judicial interpretation and adjudication generally, see Fredman, Sandra, 'Foreign Fads or Fashions: The Role of Comparativism in Human Rights Law' (2015) 64 *International and Comparative Law Quarterly* 631.

[15] For an up-to-date list, see 'International Human Rights Observations on Abortion in Ireland', IFPA, available at www.ifpa.ie/Hot-Topics/Abortion/International-Human-Rights-Observations-on-Abortion-in-Ireland.

[16] For recent summaries of relevant international human rights law, see Christina Zampas, evidence to the Joint Committee on the Eighth Amendment to the Constitution, 4 October 2017; see also 'Human Rights and Equality Considerations in the Development of a New Legislative and Regulatory Framework on Abortion', Irish Human Rights and Equality Commission, 4 October 2017, available at www.ihrec.ie/documents/human-rights-equality-considerations-development-new-legislative-regulatory-framework-abortion.

constitutional rights. Instead, courts could build on international human rights law to understand constitutional rights during pregnancy in the same way as they draw on any other persuasive sources when undertaking constitutional interpretation. They would consider the meaning, fit and impact of applying a common international approach in interpreting the Constitution. They would exercise their judgement as to whether the Constitution could properly be said to match, or even exceed, international commitments. They might well decide, in a particular case, that Irish constitutional protections in pregnancy are much more limited than those provided for under a given international human rights treaty, or that the provisions of an international human rights treaty subvert the proper meaning of the constitutional text. Thus, they may refuse to follow a treaty in interpreting the constitution. Any remaining conflict between international and constitutional law, then, could only be resolved by once again changing the Constitution by referendum.

What constitutional rights might pregnant people have?

In this section, we engage with pregnant people's rights under the Irish Constitution after removal of the 8th Amendment, drawing on developments in international human rights law as an interpretive aid. As discussed in Chapter 1, while these rights will have an obvious application in the context of abortion regulation, they will also be relevant to the protection of rights during pregnancy where no abortion is sought. Our aim here is not to provide a comprehensive overview of the applicable constitutional law,[17] but to sketch possibilities for future constitutional argument on behalf of pregnant people.

---

[17] For example, we do not consider arguments related to the right to liberty, or the right to freedom of conscience in detail here.

The right to life

The 8th Amendment explicitly pits the right to life of the pregnant person against the equal right to life of the unborn. Other than in pregnancy, the right to life, expressly protected in Article 40.3.2 of the Constitution, is not restricted in this way. That Article requires the state to 'by its laws protect as best it may from unjust attack and ... vindicate the life ... of every citizen'. With the 8th Amendment repealed, pregnant people would again enjoy the ordinary right to life under Article 40.3.2. We could use this right to argue that any legislation that severely restricts access to abortion, whether by criminalisation or otherwise, is unconstitutional.

In *McGee v Attorney General*,[18] decided 10 years before the 8th Amendment, the Supreme Court held that a woman whose health made pregnancy dangerous for her could not have her life put at risk by the laws of the state. Accordingly, Walsh J. held that the state was both required to make exceptions to its general prohibitions on access to contraception for women in her position, and positively obliged to assist women in that position to access the contraception needed to avoid putting their life in jeopardy. *McGee* is not an abortion case; indeed, the court was quite clear that 'any action on the part of either the husband and wife or the State to limit family sizes by endangering or destroying human life must necessarily not only be an offence against the common good but also against the guaranteed personal rights of the human life in question'.[19] However, a great deal has changed since *McGee* was decided. In particular, the Irish people have become more accepting of abortion, and the international consensus on the permissibility of abortion has shifted dramatically. In the absence of the 8th Amendment, we could argue by analogy with *McGee* that a person whose pregnancy poses a threat to her life has a constitutional right to legal and practically accessible abortion, and to positive state assistance in accessing it. Importantly, after the 8th Amendment this

---

[18] *McGee v Attorney General* [1974] IR 284, *per* Walsh J. at 315.
[19] *McGee v Attorney General* [1974] IR 284, *per* Walsh J. at 312.

exception should not be confined to those whose life is at 'real and substantial risk': that intolerably high threshold is a product of the 8th Amendment as interpreted in the *X* case.[20] International human rights law recognises a potential violation of the right to life where legal restrictions on abortion access compel women to undergo dangerous clandestine abortions,[21] exposing them to risky medical procedures, or requiring them to forego treatment for life-threatening illnesses.[22] This broader argument could be used to require more significant liberalisation of abortion access beyond the narrow 'right to life' exception currently provided in Irish law.

Removing the 8th Amendment would also allow us to think about the right to life beyond the simple biological condition of 'avoiding death'. Instead, the right to life could be read consistently with pregnant people's other constitutional rights. This might mean, in particular, that the Constitution could no longer support a strict distinction between life and health.[23] So, for example, arguments for the liberalisation of abortion access could be rooted in the acknowledgement that a woman's right to life is engaged even where she survives pregnancy but suffers serious damage to her physical and mental health.

The right to bodily integrity and the right to health

The right to bodily integrity is one of the unenumerated (implied) rights in Irish Constitution. It was originally developed in *Ryan v Attorney General*.[24] In *Ryan*, the Supreme Court held that the state could not, without justification, directly impose harmful treatment

---

[20]   *Attorney General v X* [1992] 1 IR 1.

[21]   See, for example, UNHRC, *CCPR General Comment No. 28: Article 3 (The Equality of Rights Between Men and Women*, CCPR/C/21/Rev.1/Add.10, 29 March 2000.

[22]   *Ramírez Jacinto v Mexico*, Case 161/02, Inter-American Commission on Human Rights, Report No. 21/07, OEA/Ser.L/V/II.130, doc. 22, rev. 1 (2007); see also brief discussion in Chapter 1.

[23]   See further Fletcher, Ruth, 'Judgment: *Attorney General v X'* (see note 2).

[24]   *Ryan v Attorney General* [1965] IR 294.

or processes on the body or endanger citizens' health.[25] The right to bodily integrity is not an absolute right; the state can make policies that have effects on our control of our bodies or health; however, any interference with that right must be proportionate and 'for the good of the whole' society.[26] The right to bodily integrity is a negative right: a right to freedom from external interference. At an individual level, it takes the form of a right to refuse consent to medical treatment.[27] As discussed in Chapter 1, pregnant people's right to refuse consent is limited by the 8th Amendment.[28] After removal of the 8th Amendment, this would have to change. More broadly, the right to bodily integrity requires that the state should desist from any actions that disproportionately interfere with pregnant people's capacity to protect their health. For example, we could argue that the state is required to decriminalise abortion. To the same effect, regard for bodily integrity might require the state to take action to prevent private acts that unreasonably obstruct access to abortion (such as the provision of inaccurate information by fraudulent crisis pregnancy agencies, or harassment and intimidation by anti-abortion activists).[29]

This interpretation of the right to bodily integrity chimes with the right to health under international human rights law. Under international human rights law, states must take measures to 'liberalize restrictive abortion laws; to guarantee women and girls access to safe abortion services and quality post abortion care … and to respect the right to women to make autonomous decisions about their sexual

---

[25] *Ryan v Attorney General* [1965] IR 313.

[26] *Ryan v Attorney General* [1965] IR 313.

[27] See *Re a Ward of Court (withholding medical treatment) (No 2)* [1996] 2 IR 79; *JM v Board of Management of St Vincent's Hospital* [2003] 1 IR 321. That right would also include the right to refuse consent to abortion: *SPUC v Grogan* [1989] IR 753, 767.

[28] Health Service Executive, *National Consent Policy* (2014, revised May 2016), p 41.

[29] *The People (Director of Public Prosecutions) v JT* (1988) 3 Frewen 141; we discuss access to abortion care, including to abortion information, in more detail in Chapter 4.

and reproductive health' in order to vindicate the right to health.[30] The right to health (including the right to sexual and reproductive health)[31] implies state obligations of non-interference. This means that states must remove any and all barriers to pregnant people's right to control of their own health, including barriers interfering with access to health services, education and information.

However, the right to bodily integrity in Irish constitutional law is narrower than the international right to health.[32] In particular, the existing constitutional right to bodily integrity cannot, thus far, be stretched to require the state to provide particular services, or kinds of medical treatment.[33] This is consistent with the general principle of Irish constitutional law that matters of socioeconomic policy are left

---

[30] United Nations Committee on Economic, Social and Cultural Rights (UNCESR), *General Comment No. 14: The Right to the Highest Attainable Standard of Health (Article 12 of the International Covenant on Economic, Social and Cultural Rights)*, E/C.12/2000/4, 11 August 2000, 8; UNCESCR, *General Comment No. 22: The Right to Sexual and Reproductive Health (Article 12 of the International Covenant on Economic, Social and Cultural Rights)*, E/C/12/GC/22, 2 May 2016, 28; UNCESCR, *Concluding Observations on the Third Periodic Report of Ireland*, E/C.12/IRL/Co/3, 8 July 2015, 30; UNCEDAW, *Concluding Observations on the Seventh Periodic Report of The United Kingdom of Great Britain and Northern Ireland*, CEDAW/C/GBR/CO/7, 30 July 2013, 50-51.

[31] United Nations Committee on the Rights of the Child (UNCRC), *General Comment No. 20: The Implementation of the Rights of the Child During Adolescence*, CRC/C/GC/20, 6 December 2016; United Nations Women, Division for the Advancement of Women, *CEDAW General Recommendation No. 24: Article 12 of the Convention (Women and Health)*, A/54/38/Rev.1, 1999.

[32] See generally Murphy, Therese, *Health and Human Rights* (2013, Hart Publishing).

[33] See further Madden, Deirdre, *Medicine, Law and Ethics* (3rd edn) (2016, Bloomsbury Professional); cf *O'Brien v Wicklow UDC* (unreported, High Court, 10 June 1994); *The State (C) v Frawley* [1976] IR 365, 372 and 374. See similarly the finding in *In the Matter of Article 26 of the Constitution and the Health (Amendment) (No. 2) Bill 2004* [2005] 1 IR 105 that there is no constitutional right to health that could ground free access to healthcare

to the government.[34] After repeal of the 8th Amendment, however, the state would be entirely free to legislate for and fund comprehensive abortion care services, even if the Constitution did not compel it to do so.

The right to privacy and self-determination

The Constitution protects the rights to individual and to marital privacy, both of which might be developed following repeal of the 8th Amendment. Privacy is not an unlimited right. The state may interfere with it for the purposes of the vindicating others' rights, or in the interests of the 'common good',[35] but such limitations must be carefully drawn. The right to marital privacy is to be enjoyed with 'possibly the rarest of exceptions'.[36] Moreover, the right to individual privacy cannot be restricted simply because a person might engage in an activity that the majority of people think is immoral or distasteful.[37]

Read together with the right to bodily integrity,[38] the right to privacy points towards a right to medical self-determination.[39] This arguably includes a right to make decisions about whether to become and stay pregnant.[40] Although the Supreme Court in *McGee*[41] held that the right to marital privacy did not include a right to access

---

[34] See more recently *MEO v MJELR* [2012] IEHC 394.

[35] *MEO v MJELR* [2012] IEHC 394.

[36] See similarly Article 8, European Convention on Human Rights; *Niemitz v Germany* [1992] ECHR 80; *X v Iceland* [1976] ECHR 7.

[37] *McGee v Attorney General*, 322 (see note 10); *Norris v Attorney General* [1984] IR 36, 71.

[38] On non-consensual obstetric treatment or examination as violating the right to private and family life under the European Convention on Human Rights, see *YF v Turkey* App. No. 24209/94, ECHR (22 July 2003); *Konovalova v. Russia* [2016] ECHR 248.

[39] UNCESCR, *General Comment No. 22*, [28] (see note 29); UN Women, Fourth World Conference on Women 1995, Beijing Declaration and the Platform for Action, [96].

[40] UNCESCR, *General Comment No. 22*, [28] (see note 29).

[41] *McGee v Attorney General* (see note 10).

abortion, much has changed since then, and the comments in *McGee* do not preclude the development of the constitutional right to privacy in order to require the decriminalisation of abortion and the liberalisation of abortion law. This is not least because international human rights bodies recognise that restrictive abortion laws infringe pregnant people's privacy,[42] dignity and autonomy.[43]

If the constitutional right to privacy were to develop in accordance with international human rights law, the state would be required, at a minimum, to ensure that any new abortion law passed was effective and accessible.[44] As we discuss in Chapter 4, this includes taking measures to avoid delays in accessing treatment, and ensuring that certification or qualification processes are transparent and do not make women 'dependent on the benevolent interpretation'[45] of restrictive or uncertain laws.

The right to be free from torture, inhuman and degrading treatment or punishment

The courts recognised a constitutional right to be free from torture, inhuman and degrading treatment or punishment in *The State (C) v Frawley*.[46] As in international law, this right is not focused solely on

---

[42] *A, B and C v Ireland* (see note 9); *Tysiqc v Poland* [2007] ECHR 219, [106]-[107]; *RR v Poland* [2011] ECHR 828, [181]; *KL v Peru*, CCPR/C/85/D/1153/2003, 22 November 2005, [6.3]; UNHRC, *Concluding Observations on the Fourth Periodic Report of Ireland*, CCPR/C/IRL/CO/4, 19 August 2014, [9]; *Mellet v Ireland*, [7.8] (see note 9).

[43] See, for example, United Nations General Assembly, *Interim Report of the Special Rapporteur on the Right of Everyone to the Enjoyment of the Highest Attainable Standard of Physical and Mental Health*, A/66/254, 3 August 2011, [21].

[44] *A, B and C v Ireland* (see note 9); we discuss access to abortion care in a practical sense in Chapter 4.

[45] UNCEDAW, *Concluding Observations of the Committee on the Elimination of Discrimination Against Women: New Zealand*, CEDAW/C/NZL/CO/7, 27 July 2012, [34]-[35].

[46] [1976] IR 365.

physical harms. It also encompasses a right to be free from serious psychological harm and degradation.[47] In Article 40.3.2 of the Constitution, the state commits to vindicate the person of every citizen; to protect the body, mind and personality of every individual.[48] This includes an obligation to treat every person with dignity.[49] The Irish courts have interpreted this obligation restrictively.[50] They place particular emphasis, not on the harmful consequences of a state policy, but on the intention with which it was done. In practice, this means that it will be difficult to establish a violation of the right to freedom from inhuman and degrading treatment, since the state can always claim that its purpose was not to punish or harm the suffering individual, and that their suffering was the indirect consequence of an attempt to pursue some more benign goal.

International human rights law takes a more expansive approach to this right. At an individual level, it recognises that subjecting a pregnant person to medical treatment without their consent can constitute inhuman and degrading treatment,[51] and that the right is violated if the *effect* of the treatment was to humiliate and degrade, whether

---

[47] See, for example, *Pretty v United Kingdom* [2002] 35 EHRR 1, [51]; *Ireland v United Kingdom* [1980] 2 EHRR 25, [52]; UNCAT, *General Comment No. 3: Implementation of Article 14 by States Parties*, CAT/C/GC/3, 13 December 2012, [3].

[48] *Kinsella v Governor of Mountjoy Prison* [2011] IEHC 235; *The State (Richardson) v Governor of Mountjoy Prison* [1980] ILRM 82.

[49] *Kinsella v Governor of Mountjoy Prison* [2011] IEHC 235; *The State (Richardson) v Governor of Mountjoy Prison* [1980] ILRM 82.

[50] It is worth noting that the right has most often been invoked in imprisonment cases, which, unfortunately, may explain judicial reluctance to extend it.

[51] On subjecting women to obstetric treatment or examination without consent as inhuman and degrading treatment, see *VC v Slovakia* [2011] ECHR 1888; *NB v Slovakia* [2012] ECHR 991; *IG v MK and RH v Slovakia* [2012] ECHR 1910; *RR v Poland* [2011] ECHR 828; Center for Reproductive Rights, *Reproductive Rights Violations as Torture and Cruel, Inhuman, or Degrading Treatment or Punishment: A Critical Human Rights Analysis* (2011). On torture in healthcare settings more generally, see UNHRC, *Report of the Special Rapporteur on Torture and Other Cruel, Inhuman or Degrading Treatment*, Juan E. Méndez, A/HRC/22/53, 1 February 2013, [10]-[11].

or not that was the practitioner's intention.[52] Furthermore, states are required both to refrain from inhuman and degrading treatment in their own institutions, and to take steps to prevent its imposition by others.[53] This obligation is absolute;[54] there are no exceptions, and no defences.[55]

If we move away from the question of direct medical treatment to the broader issue of legislative prohibitions on abortion, international human rights law is also very useful. It acknowledges that restrictive abortion law may breach pregnant people's rights to freedom from cruel, inhuman or degrading treatment. The United Nations Committee on the Elimination of all forms of Discrimination against Women (UNCEDAW) has said that the criminalisation, denial or delay of safe abortion or post-abortion care are 'forms of gender-based violence that ... may amount to torture or cruel, inhuman or degrading treatment'.[56] This may be because a pregnant person is often exposed to dangerous abortion procedures where abortion is not otherwise legal. However, international human rights law also recognises that being compelled to continue a pregnancy where abortion is inaccessible may, in itself, constitute torture, inhuman or degrading treatment or punishment. This is because requiring a pregnant person to continue a pregnancy after rape,[57] where that individual's own health is at risk,

---

[52] *VC v Slovakia* (see note 50). See also UNHRC, A/HRC/22/53, 1 February 2013, [5] (note 50).

[53] See, for example, UNCAT, CAT/C/GC/3, 13 December 2012, [5], [18], [23], [37], [39] (note 46).

[54] Mavronicola, Natasa, 'Is the Prohibition Against Torture and Cruel, Inhuman and Degrading Treatment Absolute in International Human Rights Law? A Reply to Steven Greer' (2017) 17(3) *Human Rights Law Review* 479.

[55] UNCAT, *Concluding Observations on the Second Periodic Report of Ireland*, CAT/C/IRL/CO/2, 31 August 2017, [31].

[56] UNCEDAW, *General Recommendation No. 35 on Gender-based Violence Against Women, updating General Recommendation No. 19*, CEDAW/C/GC/35, 14 July 2017, [1] and [31(a)].

[57] UNCAT, *Consideration of Reports Submitted by States Parties under Article 19 of the Convention. Concluding Observations of the Committee Against Torture: Nicaragua*, CAT/C/NIC/CO/1, 10 June 2009, [16].

or where the foetus is severely impaired,[58] may expose women to severe trauma and anguish.[59] The United Nations Human Rights Committee confirmed this position in two recent cases against Ireland; *Mellet* and *Whelan*.[60] A key point from these cases is that allowing pregnant people to travel to access abortion abroad does not sufficiently vindicate this right. In requiring women to travel to access abortion abroad, on their own, without any significant economic, medical or emotional support, the state exacerbates the violation caused by criminalising abortion in the first place. The state's neglect, in this instance, can violate women's rights.[61]

The right to equality

Abortion access also raises questions for the constitutional guarantee of equality.[62] Restrictive abortion laws discriminate against women.[63] As we have seen in our discussion of the right to life and the right to bodily integrity, restrictive abortion laws mean that pregnant women cannot enjoy other fundamental rights in the same ways as men do.[64]

---

[58] *Mellet v Ireland* (see note 9); *Whelan v Ireland*, [7.7] (see note 9). See note 50.

[59] *Mellet v Ireland*, [7.4] and [7.6] (see note 9); *Whelan v Ireland*, [7.7] (see note 9). See also *P and S v Poland,* No. 57375/0 ECtHR (2012); *KL v Peru* (see note 41); UNHRC, CCPR/C/IRL/CO/4, 19 August 2014 (see note 41).

[60] *Mellet v Ireland* (see note 9); *Whelan v Ireland* (see note 9).

[61] *Mellet v Ireland* (see note 9). See similarly *The State (C) v Frawley* [1976] IR 365, 372 noting that the right may be breached by omission. Contrast *In the matter of an application by the Northern Ireland Human Rights Commission* [2017] NICA 42, currently awaiting judgment from the UK Supreme Court.

[62] McGuinness, Sheelagh and Widdows, Heather, 'Access to Basic Reproductive rights: Global Challenges', in Francis, Leslie (ed) *The Oxford Handbook of Reproductive Ethics* (2016, OUP).

[63] UNHRC, *Consideration of Reports Submitted by States Parties Under Article 40 of the Covenant. Concluding Observations by the Human Rights Committee: Peru*, CCPR/CO/70/PE, 15 November 2000, [20].

[64] United Nations General Assembly, *Interim Report of the Special Rapporteur on the Right of Everyone to the Enjoyment of the Highest Attainable Standard*

Ensuring access to abortion helps to create the conditions in which women can plan their families. This in turn contributes to addressing the entrenched gender inequality associated with uneven distribution of childcare responsibilities.

The 8th Amendment produces and reflects wider inequalities in Irish society. Whatever the Constitution says, women with money can usually access safe abortion when they need to; women without money often cannot. Indeed, the United Nations Human Rights Committee recently held that Ireland's current law discriminates on socioeconomic grounds, because wealth has such a significant impact on the ability to exercise reproductive autonomy in Ireland.[65] In Ireland—as elsewhere—people without money are more often than not people who experience a wide variety of other intersecting inequalities. They may be asylum seekers, Travellers, women of colour, disabled people, children, or LGBTQI* people. They may live in inaccessible parts of the country with poor public transportation links and limited broadband access. Their lack of reproductive autonomy will not be fully addressed by expanding constitutional rights to privacy, bodily integrity, or freedom from torture, inhuman and degrading treatment or punishment. Rather, as we discuss at the end of this chapter, a substantive and rich conceptualisation of equality, and an associated commitment to reproductive justice, is needed to fully realise their rights to access abortion—even in a post-repeal Ireland.[66]

The Constitution could be part of that project. It contains a right to equality,[67] which the Supreme Court has recognised as going 'to the essence of human personality'.[68] According to Article 40.1, that

---

of Physical and Mental Health, A/66/254, 3 August 2011, [16] and [34].

[65] *Mellet v Ireland* (see note 9).

[66] Culhane, Leah, 'Reproductive Justice and the Irish Context: Towards an Egalitarian Framing of Abortion' and Sherlock, Leslie, "Towards a Reproductive Model of Reproductive Justice in Ireland', both in Quilty, Aideen et al (eds) *The Abortion Papers Ireland: Volume 2* (2015, Cork University Press).

[67] Article 40.1, Constitution of Ireland.

[68] *NVH v MJELR*, [10] (see note 10).

guarantee of equality 'shall not be held to mean that the State shall not in its enactments have due regard to differences of capacity, physical and moral, and of social function'.[69] This is a simple acknowledgement that to treat everyone the same is not to ensure equality. It can be interpreted restrictively: we might say that people who get pregnant should be required to stay pregnant, even at considerable cost to themselves, because this is their 'natural' 'physical function', and the state has no obligation to correct this. In *Mellet*, the United Nations Human Rights Committee called this the 'stereotypical idea that a pregnant woman should let nature run its course, regardless of the suffering involved for her'.[70] We could move away from that stereotype and recognise that those who can get pregnant not only have different physical and social functions, but different needs if they are to fulfil those functions with dignity and without unnecessary suffering. That interpretation would require ensuring access to lawful abortion.

International human rights law can help us to envisage that shift in interpretation. Under international human rights law, women are entitled not only to equal access to the same health services as men, but also to access to gender-specific healthcare where required.[71] Restricting abortion access constitutes gender discrimination in

---

[69] Article 40.1, Constitution of Ireland.

[70] Sarah Cleveland, individual opinion in *Mellet v Ireland* (see note 9).

[71] United Nations Women, Division for the Advancement of Women, A/54/38/ Rev.1, 1999, [11] (see note 30); UNCESCR, *Substantive Issues Arising in the Implementation of the International Covenant on Economic, Social and Cultural Rights. General Comment No.16: The Equal Right of Men and Women to the Enjoyment of All Economic, Social and Cultural Rights (Article 3 of the International Covenant on Economic, Social and Cultural Rights)*, E/C. 12/2005/4, 11 August 2005, [29]. On discrimination and obstetric violence, see also *Alyne da Silva Pimentel Teixeira* (deceased) *v Brazil*, UNCEDAW, *Views: Communication No. 17/2008*, CEDAW/C/49/D/17/2008, 10 August 2011. See further UNHRC, A/HRC/22/53, 1 February 2013, [7]-[8] (note 50). The European Court of Human Rights has been reluctant to accept that obstetric violence is often associated with discrimination against women, or particular categories of women; see, for example, Roma sterilisation cases such as *VC v Slovakia* (note 50).

healthcare both because abortion is a procedure that only women need and because compelling women to continue a pregnancy exposes them to gender-specific health risks.[72] Prohibiting abortion reduces women to potential mothers, thus perpetuating gender-based stereotypes. In Nigel Rodley's words, our abortion law sends the message that a woman is 'a vessel and nothing more'.[73] Ireland has an obligation to progress women's social position by modifying 'social and cultural patterns' of bias in order to eliminate gendered prejudices and stereotypes.[74] If, as we have argued, the 8th Amendment reinforces those stereotypes in Irish constitutional law and medico-legal practice, addressing this will require more than repeal. It will require a wholesale reorientation of abortion law. Recognising access to abortion as being fundamentally grounded in equality would go some way towards achieving that.[75]

An outline of pregnant people's constitutional rights after the 8th

We argue that without the 8th Amendment the constitutional case for decriminalisation of abortion is clear, not only in exceptional or 'deserving' cases, but in all cases where women might need abortions, on equality and privacy grounds. A continuing prohibition on abortion access will be difficult to sustain in cases of risk to life, serious risk to health, fatal foetal abnormality and rape. The case for these exceptions to any general prohibition is rooted in the constitutional rights to life and freedom from torture, inhuman and degrading treatment. Once those legislative exceptions are in place, arguments for the right to privacy suggest that illegitimate obstacles to abortion access

---

[72] United Nations Women, Division for the Advancement of Women, A/54/38/Rev.1, 1999 (see note 30). UNHRC, Report of the Working Group on the Issue of Discrimination against Women in Law and in Practice, A/HRC/32/44, 8 April 2016 [23]; concurring opinions of Sarah Cleveland, Yadh Ben Achour, Victor Manuel Rodríguez Rescia, Olivier de Frouville and Fabián Omar Salvioli in *Mellet v Ireland* (see note 9).

[73] UNHRC, CCPR/C/IRL/CO/4, 19 August 2014 (see note 41).

[74] Article 5, Convention on the Elimination of Discrimination Against Women.

[75] McGuinness, Sheelagh and Widdows, Heather (see note 61).

must be removed; if abortion is made legal, it must also be practically accessible. Furthermore, without the 8th Amendment, respect for the right to bodily integrity means that it will be much more difficult to legitimate coercive medical treatment of pregnant people, both within and outside the abortion context. In order to give effect to these rights, people whose pregnancies are likely to be very difficult and distressing—because they are affected by serious medical risks, rape or serious foetal anomaly—will have a strong claim to the information and support necessary to minimise their pain and anguish. It is possible to go further and to make a broader claim for abortion rights on behalf of pregnant people who not come within the scope of these 'exceptions'.[76] A general constitutional right to self-determination in matters of reproduction, established under the heads of the right to privacy and the right to equality, could be developed and applied, not only to buttress a right to access abortion in exceptional circumstances, but to justify legislating for abortion access for all pregnant people who need it.

It seems clear, from this perspective, that the Protection of Life During Pregnancy Act 2013 (PLDPA) (summarised in Chapter 1) will not pass constitutional muster once the 8th Amendment is repealed. New abortion legislation will be required. We say this for four reasons. First, the PLDPA criminalises abortion in almost all cases. Second, it prohibits abortion even in the 'exceptional' cases where the pregnant person's health is at serious risk, where she is pregnant as a result of rape or where she has received a diagnosis of serious foetal anomaly. Third, the right to privacy is violated because the process for accessing a legal abortion in Ireland is humiliating and degrading, especially for suicidal women. The law is still very uncertain, and women are likely to experience serious delay in accessing treatment. Finally, if we take a broad reading of the constitutional position after repeal, the PLDPA, by prohibiting abortion in almost all cases, does not make effective provision for the equality and privacy rights of the majority of pregnant people who will require abortions.

---

[76] We discuss this further in Chapter 4.

After repeal of the 8th, then, the PLDPA must be replaced by new abortion legislation. As we have already noted, it is unlikely that we can make a constitutional case for 'unrestricted' access to abortion at all points in pregnancy. As we have said, the constitutional rights to bodily integrity, equality and privacy can be subjected to proportionate restrictions. The state's interest in protecting foetal life would likely permit imposing some legislative restrictions on abortion access, such as time limits, for example. In the next section, we explain how the state's interest in protecting foetal life might be used to justify some forms of abortion regulation.

Valuing foetal life in the Constitution

Under the 8th Amendment, the foetus is a constitutional rights-bearer.[77] We assume that, after repeal, this would no longer be the case. As discussed in Chapter 2, it is generally understood that the unborn has an enumerated constitutional right to life, contained in the 8th Amendment, and may have some other unenumerated rights. Some people have expressed concern that even if the 8th were repealed, those unenumerated rights would remain, and could be further developed by a court in an appropriate case, even to the point of restricting the development of new abortion legislation. We think that this risk is very small. In most states, where the constitutional text does not provide for the right to life of the unborn, constitutional courts have been reluctant to enumerate one.[78] It is difficult to imagine a circumstance in which our Supreme Court could revive unenumerated foetal rights after repeal of the 8th without utterly disregarding the electorate's

---

[77] See the discussion in Chapter 1.

[78] Where constitutions do not provide such an express right, most courts have been reluctant to create one, for example the Colombian Constitutional Court in Case T-355/06 (2006), discussed in Ngwena, Charles, 'Conscientious Objection to Abortion and Accommodating Women's Reproductive Health Rights: Reflections on a Decision of the Constitutional Court of Colombia from an African Regional Human Rights Perspective' (2014) 58(2) *Journal of African Law* 183.

intent in voting for that repeal; that is, to make it possible to liberalise Ireland's abortion law to some degree. Moreover, even if the foetus does have such unenumerated rights, they could not replicate the 8th Amendment. For example, they would not necessarily be 'equal' to the rights of the pregnant person, or eliminate her rights from consideration.

In the remainder of this chapter, we work from the assumption that the foetus should not have rights under the Constitution, but that it should have value. This is consistent with the position under international human rights law.[79] That a state does not recognise a foetal right to life does not mean that the foetus has no constitutional value. Even without constructing the foetus as a rights-bearing constitutional person, the state can assert an interest in the preservation of foetal life through voluntary and consensual pregnancy. In the Slovak Republic,[80] the Czech Republic[81] and Hungary,[82] a clear distinction is drawn between a constitutional *right* (which is not enjoyed by prenatal life) and a constitutional *value*. As the Constitutional Court of the Slovak Republic has put it, in pursuing the goal of preserving foetal life, the state cannot interfere with the *essence* of a pregnant person's rights. Women, the court held, have rights to privacy, a private life, dignity and must therefore be constitutionally protected to decide on her own 'spiritual and physical integrity': '[b]y becoming pregnant ... a woman does not waive her right to self-determination'.[83]

---

[79] See, for example, *Vo v France* [2005] 40 EHRR 12, [82]; *A, B and C v Ireland*, [227]-[228] (see note 9); *Open Door and Dublin Well Woman v Ireland* [1992] ECHR 68.

[80] Article 15(1), Constitution of Slovkia 1992 with amendments through 2014.

[81] Article 6(1), Constitution of the Czech Republic 1993 with amendments through 2002: 'Everyone has the right to life. Human life is worthy of protection even before birth.'

[82] Article 2, Constitution of Hungary 2011.

[83] Finding of the Constitutional Court of the Slovak Republic, Ref. No. I. ÚS 12/01 of 4 December 2007, published in the *Collection of Laws of the Slovak Republic* under no. 14/2008, volume 8), [13].

The rights of pregnant people are necessarily weightier than the constitutional value that is attached to prenatal life, just as constitutional rights are generally weightier than any policy goal the state wishes to pursue. Any restrictions the state wished to place on abortion access would need to meet ordinary constitutional standards. Pregnant people's rights would determine the boundaries of Irish abortion law. Restrictions on abortion access would be permitted, but must be proportionate,[84] meaning they must be rational, essential in order to achieve the state's aim, no more intrusive than the minimum necessary to achieve that aim, and otherwise proportionate to the state's aims.[85]

In other states that understand the preservation of foetal life as a constitutional value, it is permissible to limit abortion access by imposing time limits or requiring grounds to access abortion, but none of these limitations can trump all of the pregnant person's other personal rights and interests in all circumstances.[86] In the United States, the right to access abortion is constitutionally protected within the first trimester.[87] The courts have recognised that some limitations can be placed on abortion access in order to pursue the social good of preserving foetal life.[88] However, it is unconstitutional to place any

---

[84] *Heaney v Ireland* [1994] 3 IR 531.

[85] *Holland v Governor of Portlaoise Prison* [2004] IEHC 97. As discussed further in Chapter 4, it is difficult to argue that criminalisation of abortion is a rational means of protecting human life, since it does not prevent pregnant people from obtaining abortions in practice.

[86] *LC v Peru*, UNCEDAW, *Views: Communication No. 22/2009*, 4 November 2011, [8.8], [8.12], [8.15].

[87] *Roe v Wade* 410 US 113 (1973).

[88] Many US states restrict access to abortion: requiring impractical and unnecessary levels of surgical facility even for medical abortions, requiring women to access fatal heartbeat scans and undergo long waiting and reflection periods before accessing abortion care and so on. These so-called TRAP laws are frequently challenged, and sometimes struck down by the US Supreme Court. See, for example, Nash, Elizabeth et al, 'Policy Trends in the States: 2016', available at www.guttmacher.org/article/2017/01/policy-trends-states-2016; *Whole Woman's Health* v *Hellerstedt* 579 US __ (2016).

undue burdens on pregnant people's right to access abortion within that time period.[89] There is no reason why we cannot learn from other jurisdictions in adopting a proportionality-based approach to abortion access in Ireland after repeal.

It is also important to emphasise that the state can pursue its interest in preserving foetal life otherwise than by restricting access to abortion. Pregnancy is a fundamentally relational experience; the continuation of a pregnancy depends on the pregnant person's sacrifice and deep personal commitment. Concern for the preservation of foetal life within that relationship is best expressed and pursued through an empowering, adequate and effective system of reproductive justice, and not through constitutional coercion to continue with pregnancy. That system should be built to ensure that sex is consensual, that consent to sex is informed by effective programmes of sex education,[90] and that contraception is readily and freely available. Accurate and impartial abortion information should be freely available, and abortion care should be available to those who wish to access it.[91] Prenatal and obstetric medical care should be properly resourced, to preserve pregnant people's health and empower those giving birth. Child rearing should be effectively and adequately supported by the state including through the provision of adequate material support, especially in the case of those raising children on a low income.[92]

---

[89] *Planned Parenthood v Casey*, 505 US 833 (1992).

[90] Noeline Blackwell, evidence to the Joint Committee on the Eighth Amendment to the Constitution, 25 October 2017.

[91] See, for example, UNCRC, *Concluding Observations on the Combined Third and Fourth Periodic Reports of Ireland*, CRC/C/IRL/CO/3-4, 1 March 2016, [58]; United Nations Women, Division for the Advancement of Women, A/54/38/Rev.1, 1999 (see note 30).

[92] In this respect, it is worth noting that it has been difficult to invoke the 8th Amendment rights of the unborn, on its own behalf, outside of the abortion and childbirth context. For example, the state has resisted the invocation of the right in order to resist pregnant women's deportation. See Enright, Máiréad, 'The Rights of the Unborn: A Troubling Decision from the High Court?', Human Rights in Ireland, 10 August 2016, available at http://

With the 8th Amendment as our starting point, it may be difficult to imagine how this would work, but other countries have undertaken transformative changes to their abortion legislation, intended to pursue a commitment to rights and equality. South Africa is a good example. Until 1994, abortion law in South Africa was restrictive and little used;[93] instead, illegal abortion was widespread. Apartheid meant that in reality illegal and dangerous abortion was an experience almost exclusive to non-White women. In the first democratic election in 1994, the African National Congress included access to lawful abortion in its platform, and when elected passed the Choice on Termination of Pregnancy Act 1996. This Act allows for abortion on request within the first 12 weeks of pregnancy, and then introduces grounds for access after that. The further into pregnancy one goes, the more restrictive the law becomes. Counselling is never mandated, midwives can carry out abortion in the first 12 weeks of pregnancy, and no parental or spousal consent is required where a minor seeks abortion law. The preamble to the Act grounds its approach firmly in the Constitution's transformative rights regime, including rights to health, to access to fertility control of one's choice, and to the enjoyment of security in the body. Although there are continuing challenges to accessing lawful abortion, the rights-based framing of this law provides a useful example of the potential of grounding access to abortion in women's rights, and of enabling the state to limit access only where doing so respects those rights. It shows what can be done when we make the dispositional shift from reproduction as control, to reproduction as freedom. Just such a shift would be possible in Ireland after repeal of the 8th Amendment.

---

humanrights.ie/uncategorized/the-rights-of-the-unborn-a-troubling-decision-from-the-high-court.

[93] Abortion and Sterilization Act 1975.

Conclusion

In this chapter, we have begun to explore a rights-based approach to Irish abortion law. A rights-based approach is a pragmatic approach, because rights have become central ideas in pro-choice campaigns in Ireland, as around the world. A rights-based approach can fuel an important challenge to established paternalistic and punitive framings of Irish abortion law. At a political and symbolic level, the 8th Amendment subordinates everyone's agency in pregnancy to a broader 'Irish' position on the morality of abortion. [94] The state has argued before human rights bodies that the 8th Amendment 'represents the profound moral choices of the Irish people'.[95] Any new constitutional position on abortion that seeks to respect autonomy cannot enshrine, or enforce, a shared national position on the morality of abortion in all cases. Instead, the law must proceed from the position that 'hard decisions' around crisis pregnancy are ethical regardless of whether they lead to continuation or termination of a pregnancy. In the context of hard decisions, it is wrong that the Constitution as a supposed proxy for the 'will' of the Irish people takes the hard decision away from us.[96] A rights-based approach seeks to return the symbolic balance of power to pregnant people.

It is important, however, to be mindful of the limitations of a narrowly legalistic focus on autonomy-based rights in any campaign

---

[94] McAvoy, Sandra, 'Vindicating Women's Rights in a Foetocentric State: The Longest Irish Journey', in Giffney, Noreen and Shildrick, Margrit (eds), *Theory on the Edge*, (2013, Palgrave Macmillan); Fletcher, Ruth, 'Reproducing Irishness: Race, Gender and Abortion Law' (2005) 17 *Canadian Journal of Women and the Law* 365; Fletcher, Ruth, 'Postcolonial Fragments: Representations of Abortion in Irish Law and Politics' (2001) 28(4) *Journal of Law and Society* 568; Hanafin, Patrick, 'Valorising the Virtual Citizen: The Sacrificial Grounds of Postcolonial Citizenship in Ireland' (2003) 1 *Law, Social Justice and Global Development*, http://elj.warwick.ac.uk/global/03-1/hanafin.html.

[95] See, for example, *Mellet v Ireland* (note 9); *A, B and C v Ireland* (note 9).

[96] See generally, Chang, Ruth 'Hard Choices' (2017) 92 *APA Journal of Philosophy* 586.

for abortion law reform. There are two central points here. First, as we have noted already, judges cannot interpret these rights unless and until an appropriate case comes to court. That opportunity may depend on the emergence of a courageous individual or individuals willing to bare private injury and trauma in public, as constitutional litigants. Thus, the courts may not have the opportunity to hear an appropriate case for years; they may not have the opportunity to do so at all. Even if cases come to court, there is always the risk that litigants' cases will be framed narrowly and strategically, and that the courts will respond conservatively, so that, for example, rights to access abortion in exceptional circumstances are upheld,[97] while other areas of abortion law are left undeveloped. So, with abortion as with so many other areas of governance, much of the ordinary work of constitutional interpretation (and of anticipating how the courts might interpret the Constitution if they had the opportunity to do so) must take place within the legislative process and associated political discourse.

In Ireland, the legislature has historically been reluctant to respond to constitutional decisions on abortion law; recall that it took more than 20 years for the Oireachtas to legislate following the *X* case.[98] Therefore, the work that Irish pro-choice activists have been doing over decades in taking ownership of rights discourse, and helping to reconceive abortion access as a fundamental right, will continue, however the courts engage with abortion in the future.[99] The struggle to build legislation that reflects emancipatory framings of that right, and translates them into concrete practice, will essentially be a political one. We need not make the courts the central focus of our discussion

---

[97] See Brown, Wendy, 'Suffering Rights as Paradoxes' (2000) 7(2) *Constellations* 208-229; Smart, Carol, *Feminism and the Power of Law* (1989, Routledge).

[98] *Attorney General v X* (see note 19).

[99] See further, West, Robin, 'From Choice to Reproductive Justice: De-Constitutionalizing Abortion Rights' (2009) 118 *Yale Law Journal* 1394; Brown, Wendy, 'Reproductive Freedom and the Right to Privacy: A Paradox for Feminists', in Diamond, Irene (ed) *Families, Politics and Public Policy* (1983, Longman).

of abortion rights, and we do not need to wait for the courts to confer abortion rights on pregnant people.

Second, as our discussion of constitutional law has shown, legal rights are blunt instruments. For example, through the rights to bodily integrity and privacy, the Constitution is now reasonably well equipped to protect a sphere of autonomy within which individuals can enjoy some freedom from state interference. Through the right to freedom from torture, inhuman and degrading treatment, it provides some protection from the worst forms of state-sanctioned violence. If the state acknowledged that pregnant people enjoyed these basic rights, Irish abortion law could be transformed. But that would not be the end of the story. The Constitution has been of much less use when individuals have sought positive assistance and support from the state, particularly in the form of the provision of social and economic resources that strengthen rights to freedom from state interference. These limitations are not only produced by the historic conservatism of the Irish judiciary; they are built into the traditional structure of liberal rights.[100] We cannot do more than sketch this argument here, but it is an old and long-established one in feminist theory.

Traditional rights discourse assumes robustly autonomous individuals who can navigate life's difficulties for themselves if the state will only remove punishments and prohibitions. Rights of this kind tend to displace responsibility for supporting pregnancy, and for child rearing, onto individuals and families, disavowing the need for broader social supports. Recognition of legal 'rights to choose', in this limited form, is no guarantee of emancipation.[101] Feminists committed to reproductive

---

[100] Menon, Nivedita, 'The Impossibility of Justice: Female Foeticide and Feminist Discourse on Abortion' (1995) 29(1-2) *Contributions to Indian Sociology* 370

[101] Rebouché, Rachel, 'Abortion Rights as Human Rights' (2016) 25(6) *Social & Legal Studies* 765.

justice[102] have long argued that most of us require more than space to make meaningful reproductive decisions.[103]

All people seeking abortions will benefit from supportive relationships of care with other people and with service providers, and some may need additional resources and assistance, especially those marginalised within the broader community because of age, disability, poverty, addiction, ethnicity, illness, sexuality or immigration status. The forms of service provision that are adequate for those of us who already enjoy a measure of power in the community may not be adequate for others. In the next chapter, therefore, we begin to set out a legislative and regulatory framework to give effect to abortion rights in Ireland, which moves beyond simply giving pregnant people space to fend for themselves, to providing enforceable guarantees of access to care.

---

[102] Erdman, Joanna, 'The Politics of Global Abortion Rights' (2016) 22(2) *Brown Journal of World Affairs* 39; Erdman, Joanna, 'Procedural Turn in Transnational Abortion Law' (2010) 104 *American Society of International Law Proceedings* 377; Ngwena, Charles, 'Conscientious Objection to Abortion and Accommodating Women's Reproductive Health Rights: Reflections on a Decision of the Constitutional Court of Colombia from an African Regional Human Rights Perspective' (2014) 58(2) *Journal of African Law* 183; Zampas, Christina and Gher, Jaime, 'Abortion as a Human Right – International and Regional Standards' (2008) 8 *Human Rights Law Review* 249.

[103] See further, Cornell, Drucilla, 'Dismembered Selves and Wandering Wombs' in Brown, Wendy and Halley, Janet (eds) *Introduction to Left Legalism/Left Critique* (2002, Duke University Press).

4

Accessing abortion care: principles for legislative design

Chapter 3 outlined possible routes to developing pregnant people's constitutional rights in Ireland after removal of the 8th Amendment. This chapter sketches how those rights could be implemented in legislation. We explain why abortion-specific legislation would be needed even if the 8th Amendment were to be removed from the Constitution. The bulk of this chapter outlines the kind of legislation that should replace the Protection of Life During Pregnancy Act 2013 (PLDPA). The Citizens' Assembly recommendations[1] form the backbone for our proposed replacement, but we amend and adapt them where necessary to give better effect to the rights that we have set out in Chapter 3. We begin with discussion of legislative provisions that ensure access to abortion, before considering the circumstances in which the Assembly recommended that pregnant people should be able to access abortions in Ireland. We depart from the punitive and

---

[1] The Citizens' Assembly, *First Report and Recommendations of the Citizen's Assembly: The Eighth Amendment of the Constitution* (2017).

stigmatising legal frameworks developed under the 8th Amendment, learning from other jurisdictions[2] and from the failures of the PLDPA.

Why legislate at all?

Achieving our goals requires a clean break with the PLDPA. Even if repeal were to be endorsed in a referendum, pregnant people's ability to actually access abortion care would not be transformed on the day that the constitutional change became law. As we showed in Chapter 3, it is quite possible that the PLDPA would be found unconstitutional following repeal of the 8th Amendment. It remains in place until and unless it is replaced or amended by the Oireachtas, or struck down by the courts in constitutional litigation. However, it will require replacement after repeal, and the sooner the better.

Readers may ask why it is not enough to remove all mention of abortion from the Constitution, repeal the PLDPA, and then decriminalise abortion and treat it like any other medical procedure[3] instead of legislating for it specifically. There is a real risk that, if the demands of the movement to repeal the 8th are translated into legislation, they may be co-opted and tamed, and old patterns of oppression may reappear in new legal clothing.[4] Without diminishing that concern, we note that only one 'developed' country—Canada— has no national abortion legislation. Its provinces have passed policies

---

[2] We rely here on the UN and World Health Organization Global Abortion Policy Database: http://srhr.org/abortion-policies/. A map of the world's abortion laws is available at www.worldabortionlaws.com/. See also Center for Reproductive Rights, *Compilation of Legal Provisions on Abortion in 46 European States* (November 2017) www.oireachtas.ie/parliament/media/committees/eighthamendmentoftheconstitution/Leah-Hoctor---Supplementary-Material---Illustrative-Chart-across-46-European-Countries.pdf.

[3] On Canada as a frequently-cited model for this approach see Fletcher, Ruth, 'Contextualising the Canadian Model: A Commentary' (6 December 2016) www.repealeight.ie/title/.

[4] Smart, Carol, *Feminism and the Power of Law* (1989, Routledge).

at local level, but access to services remains uneven,[5] despite very strong judge-made constitutional law on abortion.[6] In Ireland, in the 20 years between the *X* case,[7] and the PLDPA, equivalent difficulties emerged; pregnant people entitled to access life-saving abortions could not do so.[8] It is one thing for a constitution to say that the law on abortion has changed, but quite another to establish and defend abortion services in practice.[9]

Reproductive rights activists understand that abortion is a private matter that, ideally, should be kept between a pregnant person and their doctor. They are rightly concerned that the legal processes contained within abortion legislation can become as much tools of control, stigmatisation and exclusion as a source of empowerment.[10] Nevertheless, we must be clear-eyed about what 'between a pregnant person and their doctor' means, especially given increased public awareness of established practices in maternity care that have silenced, harmed and marginalised many pregnant people in Ireland.[11] Restoring abortion to medical control may mean enhancing access, but at some cost to human rights. 'Hard' regulatory instruments, including legislation, are helpful tools in reorienting deep-seated cultures of practice in maternity and abortion care.

---

[5] Erdman, Joanna, 'A Constitutional Future for Abortion Rights in Canada' (2017) 54(3) *Alberta Law Review* 727. For a history of the development of Canadian abortion law see Abortion Rights Coalition of Canada, *The History of Abortion in Canada*, March 2017 www.arcc-cdac.ca/postionpapers/60-History-Abortion-Canada.pdf.

[6] *R v Morgentaler* [1988] 1 SCR 30.

[7] *Attorney General v X* [1992] 1 IR 1.

[8] See the discussion in Chapter 2.

[9] See further Fletcher (note 3).

[10] Sanger, Carol, *About Abortion: Terminating Pregnancy in Twenty-First-Century America*, (2017, Harvard University Press) pp 22-23.

[11] Midwives for Choice, *Submission to United Nations Committee Against Torture (CAT) for Ireland's Second Periodic Examination under the Convention Against Torture and Other Cruel, Inhuman or Degrading Treatment or Punishment* (2017), p 5, available at http://midwivesforchoice.ie/wp-content/uploads/2017/01/MfC-Submission-to-UN-CAT.pdf at p 5.

Discussions on abortion law often begin by defining the circumstances in which pregnant people should be able to access abortion (the 'grounds' for access). This is where the Citizens' Assembly began its work. [12] However, we want to suggest that our first concern should be with ensuring than any new abortion legislation actually meets the needs and fulfils the rights of pregnant people, while allowing space for best medical practice and clinical judgment. Liberal abortion law on paper does not always translate into effective abortion access in practice, [13] and human rights bodies are clear that once abortion is

---

[12] The Citizens' Assembly, *First Report and Recommendations of the Citizen's Assembly: The Eighth Amendment of the Constitution* (2017), p 5 and p 38. The Assembly spent less time directly discussing the kinds of additional regulations that might be necessary to support meaningful access to abortion for pregnant people who came within those grounds. These are contained in the Assembly's five ancillary recommendations: (i) Improvements should be made in sexual health and relationship education, including the areas of contraception and consent; (ii) All women should have improved access to reproductive healthcare services, including family planning services, contraception, perinatal hospice care and termination of pregnancy if required; (iii) All women should have access to the same standard of obstetrical care, including early scanning and testing, irrespective of geographical location or socio-economic position; (iv) Pregnant women, throughout the country, should have improved access counselling and support facilities both during pregnancy and after abortion; (v) Further consideration should be given as to who will fund and carry out termination of pregnancy in Ireland. Although the Assembly report tells us that 'the greatest consensus' arose around these five recommendations, it also notes two further recommendations that were raised by a several members: (i) decriminalisation of abortion, including the use of the abortion pill; and (ii) recognition of and protection of women's reproductive rights and autonomy.

[13] Trueman, Karen and Magwentshu, Makgoale, 'Abortion in a Progressive Legal Environment: The Need for Vigilance in Protecting and Promoting Access to Safe Abortion Services in South Africa' (2013) 103(3) *American Journal of Public Health* 397; Berer, Marge 'Abortion Law and Policy Around the World: in Search of Decriminalization' (2017) 19(1) *Health and Human Rights* 13.

legalised it must be accessible without discrimination.[14] If a new Irish abortion law repeats old mistakes around access, pregnant people will remain exposed to old human rights abuses. [15]

Decisional security for pregnant people

As we set out at the end of Chapter 2, pregnant people are entitled to clearly defined abortion access procedures that support, rather than destablise, their efforts at self-determination.[16] It is obviously very difficult to make meaningful healthcare decisions in an atmosphere of uncertainty.

Information is key to decisional security.[17] The right to access reliable healthcare information is a fundamental aspect of the right to health.[18] Inadequate access to healthcare information may lead to delays that aggravate other human rights violations because they

---

[14] *Tysiqc v Poland* [2007] ECHR 219; *A, B and C v Ireland* [2011] 53 EHRR 13; UNCESCR, *General Comment No. 14: The Right to the Highest Attainable Standard of Health* (Article 12 of the ICESCR, 11 August 2000) E/C.12/2000/4; *KL v Peru* UNHRC, Communication No. 1153/2003 (2005). [7]; *LC v Peru*, UNCEDAW, *Communication No. 22/2009*, CEDAW/C/50/D/22/2009 (2011).

[15] *P and S v Poland*, No. 57375/08 ECtHR [168] (2008); *RR v Poland* [2011] ECHR 828, [161]; Human Rights Committee, *Concluding Observations: Ireland*, [9], CCPR/C/IRL/CO/4 (2014); Human Rights Committee, *Concluding Observations: Ireland*, A/55/40[VOL.I] (SUPP) (2000); CESCR, *Concluding Observations: Poland*, E/C.12/POL/CO/5, 2 December 2009, [28]; See also, *Report by Nils Muižnieks, Commissioner for Human Rights of the Council of Europe, Following His Visit to Ireland from 22 to 25 November 2016* (29 March 2017), [95].

[16] Erdman, Joanna, 'The Politics of Global Abortion Rights' (2016) 22(2) *Brown Journal of World Affairs* 39.

[17] Erdman, Joanna, 'The global abortion policies database—legal knowledge as a health intervention', 1 November 2017, *The BMJ Opinion*, http://blogs.bmj.com/bmj/2017/11/01/joanna-erdman-the-global-abortion-policies-database-legal-knowledge-as-a-health-intervention/.

[18] *Open Door and Dublin Well Woman v Ireland* [1992] ECHR 68, [72]; *Roche v United Kingdom* (2006) 42 EHRR 30 [155]; UN General Assembly, Report

inhibit access to needed treatment, and add to confusion and distress.[19] Although people in Ireland have a formal constitutional right to access information about abortion,[20] that right is limited and conditioned by the 8th Amendment in highly problematic ways. Human rights bodies have repeatedly criticised Ireland's Regulation of Information (Services outside the State for Termination of Pregnancy) Act 1995 (known as the Abortion Information Act) as an obstacle to accessible care.[21] Under the Act, any information that 'is likely to be required by a woman for the purposes of availing herself of services outside the State for the termination of pregnancies'[22] and 'services or … persons who provide them'[23] is strictly controlled.[24] These restrictions are matched by strict regulation of the information that can be provided by crisis pregnancy agencies,[25] and even by the criminal prohibition of doctors referring patients for abortion care abroad, regardless of how complex a woman's medical condition and care needs might be.[26] Doctors often feel that they cannot even send the person's medical records to a practitioner in another country; the patient must get their

---

of the Special Rapporteur on torture and other cruel, inhuman or degrading treatment or punishment, A/HRC/22/53 (2013)

[19] *RR v Poland* and *P and S v Poland* (see note 15).

[20] Article 40.3.3, as amended by the 13th Amendment (1992).

[21] Human Rights Committee, *Concluding Observations: Ireland* (2014) (see note 15) [9]; *CEDAW Concluding Observations: Ireland*, (9 February 2017), [43(c)] CEDAW/C/IRL/CO/6-7; *CESCR Concluding Observations: Ireland*, (22 June 2015), [30], E.C.12/IRL/CO/3. Also see Duffy, Deirdre and Pierson, Claire, Submission to Citizens' Assembly (2016), available at https://mcrmetropolis.uk/blog/what-happens-when-women-have-to-travel-abortion-care-and-lessons-from-ireland/.

[22] Section 2(a), Abortion Information Act 1995.

[23] Section 2(b), Abortion Information Act 1995.

[24] Sections 3 and 4, Abortion Information Act 1995.

[25] Section 5, Abortion Information Act 1995

[26] Section 8, Abortion Information Act 1995

own files (usually copied for them by their doctors)[27] and send or take them to an abortion care provider abroad.[28]

All of this means that when a pregnant person asks their doctor, for example, whether abortion would be in their best interests on medical grounds, the doctor cannot answer honestly according to her clinical judgement.[29] A pregnant person who is sure that she wants an abortion must listen to information about other courses of action, even if her mind is made up. An information provider cannot always be sure about what constitutes promotion or advocacy and so may tend to err on the side of caution and not say anything that might be construed as breaching the Act. At the same time, rogue agencies, which routinely promote false information about the impacts of abortion on pregnant people's health, are effectively unregulated.[30]

Although restrictions on information are routinely subverted and abortion information is widely available, it is generally presented carefully to avoid any charge of advocating or promoting access to abortion care. While the internet has made such information accessible to most pregnant people in Ireland, those without a reliable internet connection, or those who are not in control of their internet connection or unable to browse without supervision (such as teenagers, people in abusive and controlling relationships, and those in prison or direct provision), are most affected by these restrictions. The restrictions create information vacuums for some, making 'myth busting' about abortion difficult. The 1995 Abortion Information Act has produced general ignorance about the reality of abortion

---

[27] See Brendan O'Shea, representing the Irish College of General Practitioners, presentation to the Citizens' Assembly, 26 November 2016.

[28] Gerry Edwards, evidence to the Joint Committee on the Eighth Amendment of the Constitution, 25 October 2017. See also Veronica O'Keane, evidence to the Joint Committee to the Constitution, 25 October 2017.

[29] See further the submission of Doctors for Choice to the Citizens' Assembly (2016) at www.repealeight.ie/wp-content/uploads/2017/01/Doctors-for-Choice.pdf.

[30] Coyle,Ellen, 'Harris promises action on bogus agencies', *The Times* (6 April 2017)

care, with an associated impact on pregnant people's ability to make decisions about a procedure that they may not fully understand or be familiar with.

In order to vindicate human rights in pregnancy after repeal of the 8th Amendment, the state must safeguard pregnant people's access to non-directive, non-judgmental provision of medically accurate information.[31] This likely means funding independent counselling and advice services, including dedicated services for vulnerable groups and persons, as well as training medical staff to offer appropriate information. It means controlling partisan crisis pregnancy services and misleading graphic public protests, since these can also inhibit women's ability to access unbiased, accurate information. Finally, it means funding sexual and reproductive health education in schools and communities, so that pregnant people are equipped to navigate conflicting sources of information.

Once a woman has decided to access abortion care, she needs to be able to rely on timely decision making by her physician. Delay in decisions about whether a woman may access lawful abortion may be caused by deliberate procrastination, poorly resourced services, or decision-making processes that do not allocate responsibilities appropriately. A statutory obligation to make decisions on 'qualification' in a timely manner can go some way towards addressing this issue.[32] This requirement should also ensure that once a pregnant person has received confirmation that she is (or is not) entitled to a lawful abortion, she can take some time to decide what to do, should she wish to. This is an important entitlement, especially where the opportunity to access an abortion for a particular reason is time-limited.

---

[31] WHO (2012) *Safe abortion: technical and policy guidance for health systems*, pp 36 and 97.

[32] There is no such requirement in the PLDPA 2013, although medics are required to 'have regard to the need to preserve unborn human life as far as practicable'; sections 7(1)(a)(ii), 8(1)(b), 9(1)(a)(ii), PLDPA 2013.

Decisional security also requires physical security in locations where women may make their final decision about whether or not to access abortion care: surgeries, clinics, hospitals and counselling facilities. Protest actions at these locations sometimes take the form of silent vigils, but on other occasions are aggressive and intimidating. Commonly deployed tactics include calling the pregnant person 'Mum' as she passes, asking her whether she loves her baby, showing photographs of stillbirths presented as abortions, videotaping, offering free foetal heartbeat scans and masquerading as crisis pregnancy agencies, as well as outright abuse and aggression.[33] These tactics are deliberately designed to make it extremely difficult for a pregnant person to physically access abortion care, and to force her to rethink and question her decision without the provision of effective counselling and the support, accurate information and medical care that would enable her to rethink, take time, change her mind, or leave and return as she so wishes. That motivation distinguishes intimidation from care. The right to protest abortion law, or indeed any law, is not absolute.[34] In some jurisdictions, 'buffer zones' have been created near places where abortion care is provided to prohibit protest and intimidation within a certain physical distance, usually around 100 metres.[35] Such a scheme strikes a fair balance between the right of people opposed to abortion to exercise their speech and to assemble, and the right of the pregnant person to access abortion care without intimidation or distress.[36]

---

[33] See, for example, The Back Off Campaign back-off.org.

[34] *Van Den Dungen v the Netherlands*, App. No. 22838.93, 80 Eur. Comm'n HR Dec. & Rep. 147, § 2 (1995).

[35] For example in Canada, British Columbia has a fixed buffer zone of 160 metre around the abortion clinic provider (section 6(3), Access to Abortion Services Act 1995). Section 10(1) South Africa Choice on Termination of Pregnancy Act prohibits obstructing of abortion facilities and imposes 10 years of imprisonment penalty.

[36] The European Court of Human Rights has upheld states' ability to impose geographical restrictions on protest; *Ziliberberg v Moldova* (App 61821/00) Inadmissible, 4 May 2004. See also *Annen v Germany* App No 3690/10, 26. November 2015 dissenting judgments of Judges Yudkivska and Jäderblom. *Annen* is a judgment about defamation of doctors working in abortion clinics

Decisional security for pregnant people thus requires information, timely decision making about one's right to access lawful abortion care, and the physical security to make a decision without undue influence in locations where abortion care is provided. After repeal of the 8th Amendment, it is no longer the law's function to direct people away from accessing abortion care. Rather, the law's function is to enable people to make their own decisions about whether abortion is the right choice for them. This is the norm in medical law; the law should create the conditions for informed consent to medical treatment. For decades, doctors in Ireland have been constructed as the gatekeepers of access to very limited lawful abortion. Completing the shift to empowering and facilitating pregnant people to access abortion will require a wholesale reconceptalisation of the doctor–patient relationship under law.[37]

Rethinking the doctor–patient relationship: addressing stigma

Irish abortion law stigmatises the very procedure it is designed to regulate, those who seek to access it, and those medics who provide it. Stigma begins with legislative language. As with much Irish legislation,[38] the PLDPA does not use the word 'abortion'. Instead,

---

rather than about buffer zones, and did not consider the harm such protest can cause to pregnant people.

[37] In developing a non-hierarchical approach to abortion care which places pregnant people at the centre, we have a great deal to learn from the activist practices of care that have been improvised in the shadow of the 8th Amendment; for example, supplying and supporting use of the abortion pill, or providing information and material assistance to pregnant people in travelling for abortions. Rebouché, Rachel, 'The Limits of Reproductive Rights in Women's Health' (2011) 63(1) *Alabama Law Review* 1; Rossiter, Ann, *Ireland's Hidden Diaspora: The 'Abortion Trail' and the Making of a London-Irish Underground, 1980-2000* (2009: IASC Publishing); Fletcher, Ruth, 'Negotiating Strangeness on the Abortion Trail' in Rosie Harding et al (eds), *ReValuing Care in Theory, Law, and Policy: Cycles and Connections* (2017, Routledge).

[38] For use of the term see section 7 Censorship of Publications Act 1946; section 10, Health (Family Planning) Act 1979; SI No. 272/2008 European

it speaks about the 'termination of pregnancy', which, in Ireland, has been interpreted to mean all forms of bringing a pregnancy to an end, including by delivering a baby.[39] A first step towards destigmatising abortion in Irish law would be to use the word 'abortion' openly in our laws. Similarly, repeal of the 8th Amendment must be accompanied by a move away from using the current constitutional term 'unborn child' in law, and towards medical terminology (such as foetus or neonate) that avoids creating subliminal analogies between abortion and the killing of a born human being.[40] Changing our legislative language would help to normalise abortion within both legal and medical contexts and enable open, effective conversations about medical options and what might be the right course of action for the pregnant person. If decisional security relies on information, so too does it rely on honest and non-directive conversations within a balanced doctor–patient relationship. Language is more than merely symbolic; it is affective. It matters, and the linguistic choices we make mater for the stigmatisation of abortion care.

However, language alone is not enough to rethink the relationship between doctor and patient in the context of abortion care. Stigma also persists as power imbalances in the structures of abortion law. Law can subordinate pregnant people's decision making to exceptional certification and verification processes that make medical personnel, and particularly doctors, gatekeepers of pregnant people's ethical decision making. When a pregnant woman has to 'qualify' for abortion care, she is made an exception to the normal operations of medical practice; marked as someone who cannot be trusted to make weighty decisions about their own medical care for themselves, someone

---

Communities (Classification, Packaging, Labelling and Notification of Dangerous Substances) Regulations 2008; SI No 50/2016-Notification and Control of Diseases affecting Terrestrial Animals Regulations 2016.

[39] Department of Health, 'Implementation of the Protection of Life During Pregnancy Act 2013 – Guidance Document for Health Professionals' (19 September 2014).

[40] See generally Greasley, Kate, *Arguments about Abortion: Personhood, Morality and Law* (2017, Oxford University Press).

whose decisions must be overseen and, often, overridden.[41] This is important: having to justify personal reproductive choices may cause distress that exacerbates other human rights violations,[42] and may deter people from seeking abortion care even when lawfully entitled to access abortion. Stigma may also have distancing effects on those applying legislation; intimate, ethical, clinical and personal decisions become unfeeling and legalistic, and appropriate care takes second place to the strictures of formal law. Rights-based abortion law should avoid unduly burdensome access procedures[43] and afford a wide zone of trust and discretion within the doctor–patient relationship. Ideally, doctors provide care; they do not police reproductive decision making. Abortion law needs to recognise and ensure this.

This goes further than ensuring that medics facilitate abortion decision making, rather than gatekeeping abortion care. It also requires sensible and practical regulation of methods by which abortions are obtained. Ordinarily, we recognise that medical treatment is often self-administered, following consultation with a qualified practitioner, and that the severity and complexity of a patient's symptoms, history and required treatment should determine where and how they are treated.

Irish abortion law currently only permits abortion care to be provided in the 25 hospitals listed in Schedule to the PLDPA. These hospitals are chosen for their expertise in maternity care,[44] or in intensive and critical care.[45] Under the 8th Amendment, this restriction makes sense because abortion is only legal in complex, life-threatening situations. However, if abortions are provided in a wider range of circumstances, they must also be available in a wider range of settings. Sometimes

---

[41] For example Sanger, Carol (see note 10); Marzilli, Alan, *Fetal Rights* (2005, Chelsea House Publishers) pp 101-102

[42] Mellet v Ireland, Human Rights Committee, Communication no. 2324/2013 (2016), [7.4].

[43] World Health Organization, World Health Organization, Department of Reproductive Health and Research, *Safe abortion: technical and policy guidance for health systems* page 94 (2013).

[44] Section 3(1)(a), PLDPA 2013.

[45] Section 3(1)(b), PLDPA 2013.

abortions need to take place in hospitals—for example, in cases of foetal anomaly where the pregnancy is terminated by inducing labour.[46] But hospital services are not usually needed where an abortion takes place earlier in pregnancy.[47] An early surgical abortion can usually be performed up to 24 weeks of pregnancy. Before 12-14 weeks, the pregnancy is removed by vacuum aspiration, which takes five to 10 minutes, with a very short recovery time. There are few risks, and before 15 weeks a general anaesthetic is not usually required. After 12-14 weeks, dilation and evacuation will usually be used instead of vacuum aspiration. Again, this is a minor operation. It takes 10-20 minutes, with one to two hours of recovery and observation time. A general anaesthetic will usually be offered. Both of these procedures will be familiar to Irish women who have travelled abroad for abortions. Both could be provided in specialist clinics in Ireland in the future,[48] by appropriately trained midwives as well as by doctors.[49]

Under the current law, many women in Ireland, in common with women all over the world, have used the pills misoprostol and mifepristone to induce medical abortions at home, although they

---

[46] Royal College of Obstetricians and Gynaecologists, *Termination of Pregnancy for Fatal Feotal Abnormality in England, Scotland and Wales: Report of a Working Party* (May 2010).

[47] World Health Organization, Department of Reproductive Health and Research, *Safe Abortion: Technical and Policy Guidance for Health Systems* (see note 43), 15.

[48] At present, organisations offering abortion care services in other jurisdictions can be prevented from setting up clinics in Ireland, and from exporting abortion pills to Ireland, in accordance with the 8th Amendment. If the Amendment is removed from the Constitution, however, provisions of EU law on cross-border service provision may come back into force, potentially entitling foreign providers based elsewhere in the EU to establish services in Ireland. See, by analogy, Hervey, Tamara and Sheldon, Sally, 'Abortion by Telemedicine in Northern Ireland: Patient and Professional Rights across Borders' (2017) 68(1) *Northern Ireland Legal Quarterly* 1.

[49] Sheldon, Sally and Fletcher, Joanne, 'Vacuum aspiration for induced abortion could be safely performed by nurses and midwives' (2017) *Journal of Family Planning and Reproductive Health Care* 1; see, for example, sections 1(x), 4-6, 10 of South Africa Choice on Termination of Pregnancy Act 1996.

are not licensed for this purpose in Ireland. After repeal of the 8th Amendment, the state should ensure that these medicines are made available in Ireland, and that all existing restrictions are lifted. These pills are appropriate for use up to 12-14 weeks and the risks of use, especially under medical supervision, are very low.[50] Organisations like Women on Web,[51] Women Help Women[52] and Need Abortion Ireland[53] currently assist pregnant people in ordering, importing and using these pills in Ireland.[54] Medical support takes the form of 'telemedicine', that is, online and phone-based consultation with a trained volunteer or medical practitioner.[55] Use of the pills is, of course, criminalised under existing law.[56] However, people will expect to be able to continue to access abortion pills outside of a clinical setting even if Irish abortion legislation changes, and many will appreciate being able to do so locally and privately, with access to a medical examination, advice and aftercare. If abortion is to be legally available without restriction within early pregnancy, there is no reason why a person who is less than nine weeks pregnant[57] and in good physical health should not be able to access these pills with a doctor's prescription and take them at home. This approach is taken in other jurisdictions.[58] It may

---

[50] World Health Organization (see note 43).

[51] Women on Web, www.womenonweb.org.

[52] Women Help Women, https://womenhelp.org.

[53] Need Abortion Ireland https://needabortionireland.org.

[54] Sheldon, Sally, 'How Can a State Control Swallowing? The Home Use of Abortion Pills in Ireland' (2016) 24 *Reproductive Health Matters*, 90-101; Aiken, Abigail et al, 'Experiences and characteristics of women seeking and completing at-home medical termination of pregnancy through online telemedicine in Ireland and Northern Ireland: a population-based analysis' (2017) 124(8) *British Journal of Obstetrics & Gynecology* 1208.

[55] Hervey, Tamara and Sheldon, Sally (see note 51).

[56] Section 22, PLDPA 2013.

[57] World Health Organization, (see note 43), 12.

[58] In Scotland, pregnant people can take the first of two pills (mifepristone) under medical supervision, returning home to take the second (misoprostol) (Witw Staff, 'Scotland will allow women to take abortion pill at home', *New York Times*, 30 October 2017); In Canada, doctors are not required to watch

also help people in very precarious situations—for example, those in abusive relationships or those in prison or direct provision—to access abortion care safely and in a timely fashion.

Addressing stigma within abortion care requires us to take practical steps to regularise the relationship between doctor and patient in the context of abortion. This is especially important if, as is often the case, medical practitioners are also going to have a role in deciding whether and when someone can access lawful abortion under a new legislative scheme. It is essential that doctors are confident in their interpretation and application of any new abortion law, but it is also crucial that they (or their legal advisers) do not adopt needlessly cautious, narrow or adversarial, interpretations of any abortion legislation. On a rights-based approach, abortion legislation should not be interpreted restrictively with the intention of confining access to those who truly 'deserve' it. At a minimum, new legislation must be accompanied by guidance (ideally published before the legislation comes into force)[59] and integrated into medical practice through rights-based training.[60]

the pregnant person swallow either tablet (Stephanie Taylor, *Doctor calls for stop of 'demeaning' practice of watching women swallow Mifegymiso 'abortion pill'*, CBC News, 11 August 2017).

[59] The guidance on implementation of the Protection of Life During Pregnancy Act 2013 (Department of Health, 'Implementation of the Protection of Life During Pregnancy Act 2013 – Guidance Document for Health Professionals' (19 September 2014) took months to be published and, once made available, was conservative, cautious, and not centered on the rights and autonomy of pregnant persons.

[60] Training in rights-based approaches to medical care has systematically been provided in some parts of Latin America to ensure that narrowly drawn access to lawful abortion is interpreted in the most rights-compliant manner possible. On this, see, for example, Clyde, Jessie *Abortion Laws Liberalizing in Latin America, But Implementation is Slow*, International Women's Health Coalition, 25 September 2017, available at https://iwhc.org/2017/09/abortion-laws-liberalizing-latin-america-implementation-slow/.

Rethinking the doctor–patient relationship: recognising reproductive agency

Any new abortion legislation must ensure that doctors and other medical professionals are perceived, and perceive themselves, not as gatekeepers to abortion services, but as assistants to the pregnant person making an abortion decision. In order to ensure that the law operates in rights-based way, centring the agency of the pregnant person, interpretation that focuses on reducing the harm of abortion law processes is vital. There are some important steps to achieving this.

First, and consistent with respect for individual privacy, a pregnant person should not be required to disclose her case to multiple doctors. Human rights bodies have criticised states, including Ireland, that require women to receive authorisation from multiple providers before they can access an abortion.[61] While doctors may need to consult with one another on the appropriateness of treatment in a particular case, at most one doctor should be required to certify a pregnant person's entitlement to access abortion care. Furthermore, there is no reason why the person certifying entitlement to access an abortion should be a consultant in every case. In circumstances where GPs and midwives are qualified to provide abortion care,[62] such practitioners should also be empowered to certify a pregnant person's entitlement to access an abortion.

Second, the law must support participatory decision making around abortion. The PLDPA does not require a pregnant person's views to be taken into account when determining the extent and nature of

---

[61] Human Rights Committee *Concluding Observations: Ireland* (see note 15); Report by Nils Muižnieks (see note 15) 77.

[62] See, for example, sections 1(x), 4-6, 10 of South Africa Choice on Termination of Pregnancy Act 1996, and the Swedish Abortion Act 1974. For a broad overview see Berer, Marge, 'Provision of abortion by mid-level providers: international policy, practice and perspectives' (2009) 87(1) *Bulletin of the World Health Organization* 58.

a risk to her life.[63] Any new abortion legislation must ensure that the pregnant person has a 'voice' in the decision-making process, just as in any other area of medical care. Those providing abortion care must be required, not only to diagnose any relevant medical condition, but also to take account of how the pregnant person perceives her own health and circumstances, and their impact on her capacity to continue the pregnancy. Medical practitioners may certify 'qualification' for abortion care, but pregnant people must have real agency in determining whether to continue with pregnancy. This is a necessary step in attempting to recalibrate the silencing and disempowering experiences and structures of obstetric care generally (which we considered in Chapter 1).

Third, a pregnant person who asks for an abortion should not be subjected to procedures designed to test her commitment to terminating the pregnancy. In some jurisdictions, pregnant people are required to undertake procedures such as foetal heartbeat scans, getting the consent of third parties,[64] undertaking mandatory counselling, or waiting for mandatory periods before they can have an abortion for which they are legally 'qualified'. While such provisions may seem innocuous, parts of the anti-abortion movement are committed to their proliferation in abortion laws around the world in order to make abortion effectively inaccessible even where it is lawful.[65] Many European countries require pregnant people to undergo a period of reflection or counselling,[66] but these requirements open up risks of

---

[63] Peter Boylan, evidence to the Joint Committee on the Eighth Amendment to the Constitution, 18 October 2017: 'while we can describe risk as low, middle and high, it is the woman's interpretation of what the risk is to her personally that is critically important in how we deal with women who are pregnant, and that side of it really has to be taken into account'.

[64] Among countries in the Council of Europe, only Turkey requires a married woman to obtain her husband's consent.

[65] McGuinness, Sheelagh, 'A Guerilla Strategy for a Pro-Life England' (2015) 7(2) *Journal of Information Law and Technology* 283.

[66] Belgium, Germany, Hungary, Italy Luxembourg, Slovakia. For an overview see Center for Reproductive Rights (note 2).

pregnant people being subjected to biased, inaccurate or directive counselling that is intended to undermine their decision making, rather than to respect and empower them in whatever decision they come to.[67] Such requirements may also generate delays in accessing treatment. Finally, law does not impose such requirements on patients in other complex and challenging medical contexts, so neither should they be imposed in the context of abortion care.

The best way to help pregnant people to make hard choices about whether to continue with pregnancy is to ensure that adequate and accurate abortion information is available, that counselling and advice is available where sought and that medical practitioners can give honest and ethical answers based on clinical judgment when patients ask for their opinion. In other words, rather than try to reduce or prevent abortion rates through imposing 'cooling-off' processes and time periods, the state should recognise that abortion decisions are ethical, made following careful thought, and to be respected. The preservation of foetal life is best achieved through reproductive justice, not through reproductive coercion.

Conscientious objection and the refusal of abortion care

Conscientious objection refers to a medical practitioner's right to refuse to participate in medical care where they hold a moral or religious objection to doing so. It poses a particular challenge to the equalisation of the doctor–patient relationship in the context of abortion care because it allows medical personnel to deny medical treatment to patients for non-therapeutic reasons.[68] Although doctors are entitled to respect for their genuinely held beliefs about

---

[67] Hoctor, Leah and Lamackova, Adriana, 'Mandatory Waiting Periods and Biased Abortion Counseling in Central and Eastern Europe' (2017) 139 *International Journal of Gynecology and Obstetrics* 253.

[68] Fletcher, Ruth, 'Conscientious Objection, Harm Reduction and Abortion Care' in Donnelly, Mary and Murray, Claire (eds), *Ethical, Legal Ethical and Legal Debates in Irish Healthcare: Confronting Complexities* (2016, Manchester University Press).

abortion, accommodating conscientious objection should not impinge on pregnant people's rights to access care, or lead to harmful and unjustified delays or obstruction in individual cases.[69]

The PLDPA provides for a right to conscientious objection for doctors, nurses and midwives carrying out or assisting in carrying out abortions except in emergency situations.[70] Only those directly involved in performing or authorising the procedure can invoke conscientious objection. Those providing ancillary nursing care, or those working in hospital administration cannot do so.[71] The PLDPA requires that a patient refused care for reasons of conscientious objection be promptly referred to a doctor who is willing to provide treatment.[72] This obligation should be maintained in any new legislation.

State-funded religious hospitals should not be permitted to refuse to provide legal abortion care on their premises purely on the basis of religious ethos. In Ireland so many hospitals and other medical centres operate under a religious ethos that institutional bans on abortion care could be very harmful. It is true that the Constitution, under Article 44.2.5, protects religious freedom and 'denominational autonomy'. However, the provision of state-funded healthcare, unlike, for example, the development of canon law, or the celebration of religious marriage ceremonies, is not a purely religious function. In this domain, where even pregnant people who share the religion of a hospital's board members are patients as well as 'parishioners', it should not be assumed that the professed ethos of the institution trumps their rights to health, bodily integrity and freedom from inhuman and degrading treatment, or that it outweighs the consciences of pregnant

---

[69] See CESCR, *Concluding Observations: Argentina*, (2 December 2011) [22], E/C.12/ARG/CO/3; UNCEDAW, *Concluding Observations: Hungary*, (1 March 2013) [31(d)], CEDAW/C/HUN/CO/7-8; UN CEDAW, 'General Recommendation No. 24: Article 12 of the Convention (Women and Health) (1999) A/54/38/Rev.1 [11]; See also, Nils Muižnieks,(note 15), 95.

[70] Section 17, PLDPA 2013.

[71] See further *Greater Glasgow Health Board v Doogan & Anor* (Scotland) [2014] UKSC 68.

[72] Section 17 (3), PLDPA 2013.

people and the consciences of the staff willing to care for them.[73] Moreover, the general position under international human rights law is that institutions, unlike individuals, do not have consciences that can be protected by the individual right to freedom of conscience.[74] Individuals' religious freedom and freedom of conscience are adequately protected by allowing for an individual right of conscientious objection that can be exercised, or not, by medical professionals on their own terms.

Mass conscientious objection reduces the numbers of medical professionals providing abortion care, leading to 'burnout'. It may also discourage medical professionals who would otherwise willingly provide abortion care from doing so.[75] The state must ensure that individual rights are properly vindicated within institutions under its control.[76] It must take steps to ensure the availability of sufficient doctors willing and trained to provide abortion care in all hospitals and in all regions.[77] Part of this process might include conducting a 'census', at regional level, requiring medical professionals who hold conscientious objections in advance of implementation of

---

[73] See Doctors for Choice (note 29) arguing that 'The 8th Amendment forced unprofessional, unethical practice upon Irish doctors who wish to provide compassionate, evidence-based care to Irish women'.

[74] See CEDAW, *Concluding Observations: Hungary*, (note 69) [31(d)] U.N. Doc. CEDAW/C/HUN/CO/7-8; see also the Colombian Constitutional Court in Sentencia T-388/09. Under ECHR law it is established that corporate persons do not enjoy individual rights such as freedom of conscience or freedom of expression; *Company X v Switzerland* (1979) 16 DR 85; *Verein Kontakt-Information-Therapie v Austria* (1988) 57 DR 81. Contrast *Burwell, Secretary of Health and Human Services et al v Hobby Lobby Stores Inc* et al. 573 US__ (2014).

[75] See further Fletcher, Ruth (note 68).

[76] See *O'Keeffe v Ireland* [2014] ECHR 96.

[77] In *International Planned Parenthood Federation European Network v Italy*, Complaint No. 87/2012, Decision of the European Committee of Social Rights of 10 September 2013 the Committee found violations of the right to health in circumstances where such high numbers of doctors (almost 70% nationally) were asserting the right to conscientious objection that abortion was effectively inaccessible in large parts of Italy.

new abortion law to declare them to their employers, as is done, for example, in Portugal.[78] Registering conscientious objection in this way would allow advance planning of service provision. If the abortion law changes substantially, many medical professionals will find themselves facing new, and perhaps personally distressing, challenges to their consciences for the first time. Training during this period of transition must include an exploration of medical, ethical and human rights perspectives on abortion as well as instruction in best practice in abortion care.

As far as possible, people seeking abortions should be entitled to know in advance when a medical practitioner is likely to refuse them access to abortion care on grounds of conscientious objection, so that they can decide not to approach that practitioner in the first instance and thus avoid running the risk of potential distress. Medical practices, together with pharmacies where abortion medication might be dispensed on prescription, should be obliged to inform pregnant people in advance if they do not provide abortion care, or are unwilling to provide advice on abortion access. This could be done by way of clear, brief, waiting-room notices, as well as notices in any routinely distributed materials advertising abortion services, such as practice newsletters or community healthcare leaflets.[79] We suggest that this approach strikes an appropriate balance between the practitioner's right of freedom of conscience and the pregnant person's right to access abortion care.

Equal access to abortion care

As noted in Chapter 3, access to abortion is fundamentally about equality, not only between men and women but also between pregnant

---

[78] Law n. 16/2007, of April 17, on the Voluntary Termination of Pregnancy. Portugal.

[79] See further General Medical Council, 'Conscientious Objection', www.gmc-uk.org/guidance/ethical_guidance/21177.asp.

people of different gender identity,[80] age, socioeconomic means, ethnic and racial background, disability, immigration[81] or other status. This requires a legislative commitment to non-discrimination in the provision of abortion care, paying particular attention to situations where stereotyping, paternalism or safeguarding requirements might inadvertently impede access to abortion care. It may also require development of specialised care pathways for pregnant people who may need additional support to exercise their rights to access abortion care, such as those pregnant through rape, or people with intellectual disabilities or mental health difficulties that affect their decision-making capacity. A radical rethinking of our approach to capacity is essential. As we have already discussed, Irish law assumes that, in some cases, pregnant people should not have the ordinary power to make medical decisions for themselves. In other jurisdictions, where there is no equivalent to the 8th Amendment, courts have suggested that pregnancy, by itself, undermines women's decision-making capacity. These issues are compounded where the pregnant person is mentally ill or has an intellectual disability; in particular because institutions, families and carers may be reluctant to support their self-determination.[82]

It will also most likely be necessary for the state to fund the services required to ensure safe pregnancy, including abortion services where

---

[80] Under the Gender Recognition Act 2015 a person assigned a female gender at birth can be legally recognised as a man without the need for any surgical intervention, and trans* or non-binary people have the biological capacity for pregnancy.

[81] See IFPA, *Submission to the Working Group on the Protection Process* (2015) www.ifpa.ie/sites/default/files/documents/submissions/ifpa_submission_to_direct_provision_wg_march_2015.pdf.

[82] The key sections of the Assisted Decision-making (Capacity) Act 2015 have not yet been commenced. At present, a clinician may act in the 'best interests' of a person found to lack capacity. Once the 2015 Act is fully in force, persons lacking capacity must be facilitated to participate as fully as possible in medical decision-making, and may appoint a decision-making assistant or co-decision-maker.

necessary,[83] and the Minister for Heath has already indicated that in his view abortion services should be publicly funded.[84]

Regulating access to abortion for children requires a delicate balancing of child safeguarding and respect for the privacy and autonomy of younger people. We counsel against making parental consent a condition of abortion access for minors. The ordinary requirements relating to consent for minors should be followed,[85] and the usual approach to child safeguarding used to intervene where the younger person is vulnerable or where pregnancy may have arisen from an abusive or exploitative relationship. A practitioner cannot guarantee absolute confidentiality to a patient who is under 16.[86] If the practitioner believes that the pregnancy might have arisen from harmful conduct, such as sexual abuse, there is a statutory obligation to report it.[87] In particular, where a child is under 15, all sexual intercourse is

---

[83] Parliamentary Assembly of the Council of Europe, Resolution 1607, [2] and [7]; UNCRC, General Comment No.15 on the right of the child to the enjoyment of the highest attainable standard of health (art.24) (17 April 2013) [56] CRC/C/GC/15; O'Regan, Ellish, O'Keeffe, Alan and MacQuinn, Cormac, 'The State will fund abortions if people vote for change – Harris', *The Independent*, 10 November 2017.

[84] O'Regan, Ellish, O'Keeffe, Alan and MacQuinn, Cormac, 'The State will fund abortions if people vote for change – Harris', *The Independent*, 10 November 2017.

[85] Sanger, Carol (see note 10). In Ireland this requires that consent be sought from a child between the ages of 16 and 18 (section 23, Non-Fatal Offences against the Person Act 1997), although there is less legislative clarity on children under 16. For patients under 16 the Medical Council recommends that consent usually be sought from parents, although '[i]n exceptional circumstances, a patient under 16 might seek to make a healthcare decision on their own without the knowledge or consent of their parents. In such cases [a doctor] should encourage the patient to involve their parents in the decision, bearing in mind [the] paramount responsibility to act in the patient's best interests' Medical Council, *Guide to Professional Conduct and Ethics for Registered Medical Practitioners,* 7th Edition, (2009), 43.4-43.5.

[86] Section 28(6), Freedom of Information Act 1997.

[87] Section 14, Children First Act 2015.

unlawful,[88] so that a mandatory reporting obligation arguably always arises when a minor under 15 presents seeking abortion care. Ensuring equal access to abortion care for minors may require recalibrating child-safeguarding requirements. A balance must be struck between safeguarding children from abusive, exploitative and harmful sexual activity, and ensuring that children can access reproductive healthcare when they need it without being afraid that this will inevitably lead to disclosure of their sexual activity to their parents in a manner and at a time that they cannot control and when they are, in any case, likely to be under extreme personal pressure. Otherwise, there is a real risk that younger people will avoid engagement with medical practitioners and instead try to deal with their crisis pregnancies alone, perhaps using unsafe methods, or delay engagement with a medic for so long that by the time they seek abortion care their pregnancy has passed a time limit and the law no longer allows them to access it.

Decriminalisation

Decriminalisation of abortion is central to rights-based abortion law reform. Under the PLDPA, it is a criminal offence to procure an abortion for oneself, or to assist a pregnant person in terminating the pregnancy, outside of the limited grounds for lawful abortion outlined in the Act.[89] The Abortion Information Act 1995 also criminalises the distribution of information essential to accessing an abortion in certain circumstances.[90]

Although best practice increasingly seeks to regulate abortion in ordinary healthcare legislation, Ireland is far from unique in criminalising abortions.[91] It is the restrictiveness of Irish law—its failure to make significant exceptions to blanket criminalisation—that sets

---

[88] Section 2, Criminal Law (Sexual Offences) Act 2006 *as amended by* section 16, Criminal Law (Sexual Offences) Act 2017.

[89] Section 22, PLDPA 2013.

[90] Section 4, Abortion Information Act 1995.

[91] See 'Worldwide Abortion Regulations, Identified policy and legal sources related to abortion', Erdman, Joanna, 'The global abortion policies

it apart from other jurisdictions.[92] As in many other former parts of the British Empire, abortion law in Ireland is a colonial inheritance.[93] The Offences Against the Person Act 1861 criminalised abortion,[94] and the courts[95] and legislatures[96] of many former colonies that formerly shared that Act continue to be influenced by it. In some jurisdictions, defences to the crime have been acknowledged,[97] and in others (for example, Canada and parts of Australia) abortion has been decriminalised altogether.[98] The jurisdictions of the UK continue to criminalise abortion, aside from in the exceptional circumstances laid down in the Abortion Act 1967, although both politicians[99] and medics[100] have called for its decriminalisation. Although the current

---

database—legal knowledge as a health intervention', 1 November 2017, *The BMJ Opinion*, available at http://sandpit.bmj.com/graphics/2017/abort-pol/.

[92] See, for example, Cook, Rebecca and Dickens, Bernard, 'Abortion Laws in African Commonwealth Countries' (1981) 25(2) *Journal of African Law* 60.

[93] In civil law countries, prohibition of abortion is often based on the French Napoleonic code.

[94] For the history of the Act see Sheldon, Sally, 'The Decriminalisation of Abortion: an Argument for Modernisation' (2016) 36(2) *Oxford Journal of Legal Studies* 334.

[95] The judgment in *R v Bourne* [1939] 1 KB 687 has been an important influence in the partial liberalisation of abortion law in other common law countries, but was never followed in Ireland. See further Cook, Rebecca and Dickens, Bernard, 'Abortion Laws in African Commonwealth Countries' (1981) 25(2) *Journal of African Law*, 60-79.

[96] Some countries, for example Nigeria retained the Act's restrictions after independence. Cook, Rebecca and Dickens, Bernard (see note 92).

[97] For examples see Botswana (Penal Code of Botswana 1964), Ghana (Criminal Code 1960), St Vincent and the Grenadines (Criminal Code in 1988), Barbados (Medical Termination of Pregnancy Act 1983), India (Medical Termination of Pregnancy Act 1971), Israel (Penal Code 1977 updated in 2014) and most recently Sierra Leone the Safe Abortion Act 2015.

[98] See, for example, The Canada Health Act 1984. Abortion is still a criminal offence in New South Wales and Norfolk Island and Queensland in Australia.

[99] See the Reproductive Health (Access to Terminations) Bill 2017.

[100] Royal College of Obstetricians and Gynaecologists, *The Care of Women Requesting Induced Abortion: Evidence-based Clinical Guideline Number 7* (2011, RCOG).

criminal penalties under the PLDPA are disproportionately high, it is not enough under international human rights law to reduce criminal sanctions. Instead, abortion must be completely decriminalised.[101]

Criminalisation can mean that pregnant people who use abortion pills, and the friends, family, medical professionals and activists who assist them, risk prosecution. In England, criminal law on abortion has also been used by anti-abortion activists as the basis for 'sting' operations, designed to 'expose' misuse of the abortion law.[102] In Northern Ireland, people have recently been prosecuted for illegal supply of relevant medicines to a pregnant person, for purchasing medicines on behalf of a pregnant person, and for inducing an abortion using pills.[103] As far as we are aware, the last prosecution of a doctor for an abortion offence in Ireland was in 1964, and the last conviction was in 1950.[104] Some might then argue that as prosecution is rare in Ireland, criminalisation is unproblematic. However, the rate

---

[101] See UNHRC, Concluding Observations on Ireland, [9], (2014) UN Doc CCPR/C/IRL/CO/4; Human Rights Committee, General Comment 28 (Article 3) on the Equality of Rights Between Men and Women, (29 March 2000) [10] CCPR/C/21/Rev.1/Add.10,; CRC, Concluding observations on the combined third and fourth periodic reports of Ireland, (29 January 2016) [58] CRC/C/IRL/CO/3-4; Parliamentary Assembly of the Council of Europe, Resolution 1607, [7.1.sd].

[102] British Medical Association, *Decriminalisation of abortion: a discussion paper from the BMA*, (February 2017); see similarly McGuire, Erin, 'DPP will not prosecute crisis pregnancy services', (10 December 2014), *The Irish Times*.

[103] See further British Medical Association, *Decriminalisation of abortion: a discussion paper from the BMA*, (February 2017) pp 18-19.

[104] We thank Dr Vicky Conway for this point. An attempt was made to prosecute a Dublin doctor in 1998, but the DPP did not proceed. On women's historical attempts to self-induce abortions see Delay, Cara '"Poisons or other Noxious Things": Women's Illegal Abortion Strategies in Twentieth-Century Ireland,' 9 May 2014, http://historyofmedicineinireland.blogspot.co.uk/2014/05/poisons-or-other-noxious-things-womens.html and 'Tea Kettles and Turpitudes: Abortion and Material Culture in Irish History', 22 March 2016, https://nursingclio.org/2016/03/22/tea-kettles-and-turpitudes-abortion-and-material-culture-in-irish-history/.

of prosecution of the offences is irrelevant.[105] First, as we know from current Irish abortion law,[106] criminalisation itself has 'chilling effects' on medical practice,[107] which means that doctors will often adopt the most conservative possible interpretation of legislation, in a kind of pre-emptive self-defence against the possibility, however slim, of future prosecution. There are similar difficulties in Northern Ireland, even though the law there is marginally more liberal than in the Republic.[108] Second, criminalisation of abortion is heavily stigmatising. It exacerbates pregnant people's distress, and may discourage people from seeking necessary medical and emotional support, including abortion aftercare.[109] As we noted in Chapter 3, the state's interest in preserving foetal life is often better served through positive public health and welfare intervention than through criminalisation. It does not deter people from seeking abortions, whether illegally in Ireland using pills or legally abroad. In many countries, criminalisation means that pregnant people cannot openly seek abortion care, compelling them to resort to secret, and perhaps unsafe, illegal abortions. That unsafe abortion has not become a major health issue in Ireland is largely explained by its proximity to England. Finally, medical malpractice is already adequately regulated by medical professional bodies, as well as by the law of medical negligence and the general criminal law.

---

[105] For an overview of arguments for decriminalization in an English context see Sheldon (note 95).

[106] *A, B and C v Ireland* [2011] 53 EHRR 13, [254]; see also Commissioner for Human Rights of the Council of Europe, Report by Nils Muižnieks (see note 15) [82] and [92].

[107] See, for example, *A, B and C v Ireland* [2011] 53 EHRR 13, [254]; *Tysiąc v. Poland* (note 14) [116]; UNCRC *Concluding Observations: Ireland*, (1 March 2016) [58(a)] CRC/C/IRL/CO/3-4; CEDAW *Concluding Observations: Ireland* (note 21).

[108] See discussion in *NIHRC's Application* [2017] NICA 42.

[109] Sifris, Ronli, 'Restrictive Regulation of Abortion and the Right to Health' (2010) 18 *Medical Law Review* 185; Kumar, Anurdha et al, 'Conceptualising Abortion Stigma' (2009) 11(6) *Culture Health and Sexuality* 625.

The Citizens' Assembly's grounds considered

As noted in Chapter 1, the Citizens' Assembly provided its recommendations on the 8th Amendment to the Oireachtas in June 2017.[110] The Assembly assumed that a new constitutional settlement on abortion would be followed by new legislation on abortion access, broadly in line with European norms and international best practice. The Assembly's recommendations and proceedings concentrated on 'grounds' for abortion (a limited set of reasons recognised as justifying a pregnant person in accessing a legal abortion) and on associated gestational time limits.[111] Members were asked to vote on whether abortion should be available under each ground and at which gestational stage: up to 12 weeks gestation, up to 22 weeks gestation, or without any time limit. The Assembly's recommendations for legislation,[112] produced in a series of ballots, are summarised in Table 1. This indicates the percentage of Assembly members who voted in favour of each ground, and the majority in favour of the preferred time limit for that ground.[113] Often where there was broad agreement between the members that a particular ground should be included in new abortion legislation, there was some disagreement as to how late in pregnancy an individual should be able to access an abortion on that ground. However, the broad trend in the Assembly's recommendations was to recommend significant liberalisation of Irish abortion law.

---

[110] The Citizens' Assembly (see note 1).

[111] Gestational age is usually calculated from the first day of the pregnant person's last menstrual cycle, which is generally considered to occur two weeks prior to conception.

[112] The Citizens' Assembly (see note 1).

[113] The ballot can usefully be compared to a November 2017 Red C opinion poll, conducted on behalf of Amnesty International, www.amnesty.ie/wp-content/uploads/2017/10/265517-Amnesty-International-Polling-October-2017.pdf.

Table 1: Citizens' Assembly recommendations on grounds for abortion and associated time limits

Ground	% of members in favour to some degree	Time limit	% of members in favour of time limit
No restriction as to reasons	64%	Up to 12 weeks gestation	48%[1]
Risk to the health of the woman	78%	Up to 22 weeks gestation	46%
Risk to the mental health of the woman	78%	Up to 22 weeks gestation	49%
Socioeconomic reasons[2]	72%	Up to 22 weeks gestation	50%
The unborn child has a foetal anomaly that is not likely to result in death before or shortly after birth	80%	Up to 22 weeks gestation	48%
Pregnancy as a result of rape	89%	Up to 22 weeks gestation[3]	35%
Risk to the physical health of the woman	79%	None	42%
Serious risk to the health of the woman	91%	None	52%
Serious risk to the mental health of the woman	90%	None	47%
Serious risk to the physical health of the woman	93%	None	57%
The unborn child has a foetal anomaly that is likely to result in death before or shortly after birth	89%	None	69%
Real and substantial risk to the life of the woman by suicide	95%	None	61%
Real and substantial physical risk to the life of the woman	99%	None	76%

[1] 44% of the Assembly members felt that abortion should be accessible under this ground up to 22 weeks gestation.

[2] This ground was added at the request of Assembly members.

[3] This vote was decided by Chair's casting vote. 31% voted for access on grounds of rape up to 12 weeks gestation and 34% for access without time limit.

In the following section, we compare the Assembly's proposed grounds for abortion access to abortion legislation elsewhere and assess them against the principles we have already outlined.

Abortion on request up to 12 weeks

In countries where abortion is legally available on request, most abortions take place early in pregnancy. For example, most abortions in the UK (80% in 2015)[114] are performed at or under 10 weeks gestation. The same should be true of Ireland, but the necessity of abortion travel means that Irish abortions are often later abortions. Early decisions of human rights treaty bodies encouraged states to repeal absolute bans on abortion. They asked states to facilitate access to abortion in cases of risk to life, risk to health, rape or incest, and severe or fatal foetal impairment.[115] However, the development of international human rights law on abortion has not stopped there. Human rights bodies have also called on states that only allow abortion on these minimum grounds to liberalise their abortion laws, and permit access to abortion as a matter of right in the first trimester of pregnancy.[116] This position reflects a recognition that pregnant people may need abortions for reasons that are not covered by these minimum grounds.[117] If abortion

---

[114] In 2015, 3451 women with addresses in the Republic of Ireland accessed abortion under the Abortion Act 1967: Department of Health, *Abortion Statistics, England and Wales: 2015* (2016).

[115] Human Rights Committee *Concluding Observations: Ireland*, [9] (2014); CEDAW Committee *Concluding Observations: Ireland*, [43], (2017); *Mellet v Ireland* (see note 42).

[116] Human Rights Committee, *Concluding Observations: Poland*, [8], (2004); *Report of the UN Working Group on Discrimination against Women in Law and Practice*, [107(b and c)] (2016).

[117] Human Rights Committee, (note 120) [8], (2004); CESCR Committee, *Concluding Observations: Poland*, [29] (2002); CEDAW Committee, *Concluding Observations: New Zealand*, [34], (2012); CRC Committee, *Concluding Observations: Zimbabwe*, para. 60(c) (2016); CRC Committee: *Poland*, [39(b)] (2015); CESCR Committee: *Concluding Observations: Poland*, [46]-[47] (2016).

is not available legally in Ireland in the first trimester, the majority of pregnant people who need abortions will only be able to obtain them legally if they can pay for treatment abroad. Requiring pregnant people to travel discriminates against poorer women, women whose travel is restricted because of domestic violence or immigration status, and girls under the control of other family members. If abortion were genuinely accessible in Ireland on request up to 12 weeks, we would anticipate that most of those abortions would be induced with pills, often at home in private, under medical supervision. The trauma and difficulty involved in travel would be eliminated.

In providing for access to abortion in the first 12 weeks of pregnancy without restriction, the Citizens' Assembly has attempted to bring Irish law into line with international norms. Some 61 countries worldwide, most located in the wealthy developed countries of the global North and in Central and Eastern Asia, permit pregnant people to access abortion on request. In a European context, Britain stands out because it does not permit women to access abortion without proving some grounds, regardless of how early in pregnancy an abortion is sought.[118] Time limits imposed on opportunities to access abortion on request vary widely and are as low as eight weeks (for example, in Guyana) and as high as 24 weeks (for example, in Singapore).[119] The most commonly imposed time limit, especially in Europe, is 12 weeks. Several European countries, including Belgium, France, Germany and Spain, allow abortion on request up to 14 weeks gestation. Sweden permits abortion on request up to 18 weeks, and the Netherlands until viability. The Assembly recommendation falls within global and European norms.

We suggest that this recommendation be given effect in any new legislation. However, consideration must always be given to the fact that some pregnant people will be unable to make an abortion decision before 12 weeks, particularly if they do not discover the pregnancy in

---

[118] Section 1, Abortion Act 1967.

[119] Section 5(1) Guyana Medical Termination of Pregnancy Act 1995; section 4(1)(a) Singapore Termination of Pregnancy Act 1974 (revised in 1985).

time.[120] Abortion legislation must ensure that people can also access abortion later in pregnancy where necessary.

Grounds for abortion

The Assembly recommends that once a pregnancy passes 12 weeks, abortion should only be available on specified grounds, to accommodate pregnant people in especially demanding circumstances. If new abortion legislation followed the shape of the simple majority votes in the Assembly ballots, a pregnant woman would be able to access an abortion in Ireland on request (or, 'on demand'[121]) in the first 12 weeks of pregnancy. After 12 weeks gestation, she would need to provide reasons for accessing the abortion. Valid reasons up to 22 weeks gestation would include the following:

- socioeconomic reasons;
- pregnancy that is the result of rape;
- risk to the woman's physical or mental health;
- diagnosis of a non-fatal foetal abnormality.

Once the pregnancy reached 22 weeks, the range of valid reasons for having an abortion would narrow. A woman could have an abortion late in pregnancy only if:

- her physical health was at risk (which need not be 'serious' risk);
- her mental health was at serious risk;
- there was a real and substantial risk to her life, whether for reasons of physical or mental illness; or
- the foetus had been diagnosed with a fatal foetal anomaly.

---

[120] BPAS, 'Why women present for abortions after 20 weeks' www.bpas.org/media/2027/late-abortion-report-v02.pdf.

[121] On de-stigmatising the phrase 'abortion on demand' see Lyon, Wendy, 'Abortion on Demand and Without Apology' (4 October 2017) https://feministire.com/2017/10/04/abortion-on-demand-and-without-apology/.

Against exceptions-based legislation

The Assembly essentially recommended an exceptions-based model for abortion legislation. It is difficult to square an exceptions-based model with a rights-based approach to abortion care that would treat abortion care as a resource that pregnant people are entitled to access. It is a struggle to separate exceptions-based abortion legislation from inherently stigmatising narratives of 'deserving' and 'undeserving' abortions. Exceptions-based legislation can also be an obstacle to securing 'certainty' and security for abortion-seeking people unless it is interpreted appropriately. This is especially the case where grounds are drafted legalistically, and separated out from one another in ways that discourage reasonably flexible interpretation of the law. A rights-based approach might justify turning away from an exceptions-based model, and allowing abortion on one 'umbrella' ground, at least up to 22 weeks. For example, legislation could provide that pregnant people could access an abortion on grounds of risk to health up to 22 weeks and, depending on the severity of that risk, later in pregnancy. In the next section, we discuss how such a broad health ground might be formulated. Alternatively, as in parts of Australia, an umbrella ground might simply say that abortion is available where termination of the pregnancy is 'appropriate in all the circumstances', leaving the evaluation of those circumstances to the certifying doctor.[122] A flexible ground of this kind allows the certifying medical practitioner to assess the pregnant person's needs holistically, focusing on the consequences for her of denial of abortion care, rather than on whether she meets one of a restrictive list of narrowly defined conditions.

We recommend that consideration be given to permitting abortion access, at least between 12-22 weeks, on a broad, health-based ground.

---

[122] See for example Abortion Law Reform Act 2008 (Victoria), Termination of Pregnancy Act, 2017 (Northern Territories).

Time limits and the myth of 'abortion until birth'

The Assembly recommended that in some cases abortion should be available after 22 weeks, that is, up to term. Indeed, that is currently the case under the PLDPA, which has no term limit and instead focuses on foetal viability. Statutory time limits tell only part of the story of abortion availability. Even where there is no term limit, this does not mean that abortion is available up to term. In Canada, for example, federal law does not impose time limits on abortion access, but few clinics or hospitals will provide abortions after 21 weeks and then only if the pregnant person's health or life is at grave risk, or the foetus is gravely or fatally impaired.[123] When an abortion is requested late in pregnancy, all relevant circumstances should be taken into account in deciding on the best way to bring a pregnancy to an end, including by attempting live birth. However, the PLDPA, as in Ms Y's case,[124] permits a competent pregnant person who requests an abortion late in pregnancy to be subjected against her will to medical procedures designed to prolong the pregnancy or ensure a live birth. It is not clear whether this position would be constitutional after repeal of the 8th Amendment. As discussed earlier, pregnant people's autonomy must remain to the fore in medical decision making as a matter of principle.

We do not recommend an upper time limit for abortion access.

Risk to health

The Assembly proposed that abortion be available on grounds of risk to the health of the woman throughout pregnancy. The definition of 'health' is crucial, and the Assembly did not discuss this in any detail. The World Health Organization (WHO) takes a holistic approach to

---

[123] See Priaulx, Nicky, Oral evidence 'Inquiry on Abortion on the Grounds of Foetal Abnormality in England and Wales' (17 August 2013), p 39, https://orca.cf.ac.uk/50207/1/Oral%20Evidence_Parliamentary%20Inquiry%20February%202013_DisCopy.pdf.

[124] See Fletcher, Ruth, 'Contesting the cruel treatment of abortion-seeking women' (2014) 22(44) *Reproductive Health Matters* 10.

defining health that would work well within an abortion law context. It defines health as 'a state of complete physical, mental, and social well-being and not merely the absence of disease or infirmity'.[125] We argue that Irish legislation should adopt this definition of health. As we will shortly show, a pregnant person seeking to access abortion under such a broad health ground could do so on the basis of a present or anticipated risk to her physical or mental health. However, the ground could go further, allowing abortion access to be secured in cases of rape, socioeconomic need, or serious foetal anomaly *if* there is a risk that pregnancy or the prospect of continuing with the pregnancy against the pregnant person's will would affect her health, broadly construed.

Although the Assembly ultimately recommended that no distinction should be drawn between physical and mental health,[126] it also voted on each as a potential separate ground. These votes seemed to suggest that as the pregnancy progresses, a distinction could be drawn between risks to physical and mental health, so that any risk to physical health might justify abortion access after 22 weeks, but only a 'serious' risk to mental health might do so. The PLDPA similarly distinguishes between suicidal pregnant people and those whose lives are at risk from physically illness. Such distinctions are discriminatory and install an artificial distinction between physical and mental wellbeing.

Legislation should not qualify risks to health here with language such as 'serious', or the damaging 'real and substantial' inherited from the *X* case.[127] Such vague terms have no clear clinical meaning[128] and do not assist medical decision making. That the risk to health is

---

[125] Preamble, Constitution of the World Health Organization (adopted 22nd July 1946, entered into force 7th April 1948) 14 UNTS 185.

[126] In a separate ballot, taken at the request of Assembly members, 72% of the members voted that no distinction should be drawn between the physical and mental health of the woman. Nevertheless, the overall voting pattern indicated a distinction between physical and mental health. No further vote was taken to explore or seek to reconcile these differences.

[127] *Attorney General v X* (see note 7). We discussed this in Chapter 4.

[128] Erdman, Joanna (see note 17).

severe is already implicit in a request for a termination at a later stage in pregnancy.[129]

We recommend that abortion be accessible on grounds of risk to health without an upper time limit.

Socioeconomic reasons

The Assembly recommended that abortion be available for socioeconomic reasons up to 22 weeks. Twenty-six countries worldwide specifically permit women to access abortion for economic or social grounds. Some jurisdictions use this sort of ground as an alternative to legislating for abortion on request. For example, in Britain a woman can only access an abortion for one social reason: that the continuation of the pregnancy involves a risk of injury to the physical or mental health of any existing children of the family.[130] Elsewhere, social and economic grounds are more commonly used, as the Citizens' Assembly proposed, to supplement a period of access to abortion on request, that is, to keep abortion access open to a wide range of pregnant people, later into the pregnancy. For example, in South Africa, abortion is legal on request up to 12 weeks, and up to 20 weeks 'if the continued pregnancy would significantly affect the social or economic circumstances' of the woman.[131] In Norway, abortion is legal on request up to 12 weeks, and up to 18 weeks if the pregnancy, delivery or care for the child 'places the woman in a difficult life situation'.[132]

Socioeconomic grounds can provide an independent 'reason' for accessing an abortion, or they can form part of other grounds. In some countries, the statutory definition of 'health' expressly encompasses economic wellbeing, or it can be interpreted to that effect. Indeed,

---

[129] Ruth Fletcher, evidence to the Joint Committee on the Eighth Amendment to the Constitution, 8 November 2017.

[130] Section 1(1)(a), Abortion Act 1967.

[131] Section 2(1)(b)(iv) Termination of Pregnancy Act, 1996.

[132] Abortion Act, Law No. 50 of June 13, 1975, *as amended*, https://lovdata. no/ dokument/ NL/lov/1975-06-13-50?q=abortlov.

should the WHO definition of health be adopted that would be the case in Ireland too, as it includes 'a state of … social well-being'.[133] In other countries, the law expressly recognises that account should be taken of a woman's social and economic circumstances in the course of assessing any risk to her health. So, for example, in Britain, in assessing whether a woman can access an abortion on grounds of risk to health 'account may be taken of the pregnant woman's actual or reasonably foreseeable environment'.[134]

We suggest that this recommendation should be implemented in future legislation. However, we also suggest that this would be done by providing access to abortion for socioeconomic reasons under a 'risk to health' ground, as part of a broader effort to avoid the worst difficulties associated with detailed exceptions-based legislation.

Rape

The Assembly suggests that a woman who has been raped should be able to access an abortion up to 22 weeks gestation. In Chapter 3, we showed that international human rights bodies have found violations of the right to freedom from torture, inhuman and degrading treatment where women who have been raped have been compelled to continue their pregnancies.[135] Rape grounds in abortion legislation can present specific difficulties if 'proof' of rape is required as a condition of accessing abortion on that ground.[136] Some jurisdictions require women to undergo a special process to test the veracity of the rape claim, such as reporting to the police (as in

---

[133] Preamble (see note 125).

[134] Section 1(2) Abortion Act 1967.

[135] *Conclusions and Recommendations of the Committee Against Torture*, CAT/C/NIC/CO/1 (2009). See also UNCAT, *Consideration of Reports Submitted by States Parties under Article 19 of the Convention: Concluding Observations of the Committee Against Torture: Nicaragua*, CAT/C/NIC/CO/1, 10 June 2009, [16].

[136] Rape Crisis Network Ireland Submission to Citizens' Assembly (2016).

the Isle of Man),[137] certification by an official in the criminal justice system (as in Poland),[138] or commencement of prosecution. However, no medical test can provide proof of rape and, of course, a pregnant person should not have to meet a criminal standard of proof (beyond reasonable doubt) to secure access to abortion. A rape trial and the provision of an abortion for reasons of rape must remain completely separate processes. In addition, given existing difficulties around the reporting and prosecution of sexual violence, any specific proof procedure is likely to lead to serious delays in access to healthcare, as well as to distress and degradation. A health ground appropriately defined in line with the WHO definition considered earlier should allow for access to abortion in cases of rape.

We suggest that this recommendation be implemented in future legislation. However, we also suggest that access to abortion be provided to people who have been raped under a 'risk to health' ground, as part of a broader effort to avoid the worst difficulties associated with detailed exceptions-based legislation.

Foetal anomaly

The Assembly recommended that abortion be accessible up to 22 weeks where the foetus has been diagnosed with a 'non-fatal foetal anomaly', and up to term if it has been diagnosed with a 'fatal foetal anomaly'. The scope of the first recommendation is not entirely clear. The Assembly did not spend a lot of time considering or hearing expert evidence on issues around foetal impairment and abortion, or indeed on disability and abortion. We assume that this recommendation concerns conditions where a live baby will be born, but will have a very short life, or one that is marked by very severe, untreatable or irreversible illness.

Under the Assembly's recommendations, abortion would be available for non-fatal foetal anomaly up to 22 weeks, and for fatal foetal anomaly

---

[137] Termination of Pregnancies (Medical Defences) Act 1995.

[138] See, for example, *P and S v Poland* (note 19).

after that period. The Irish support group Termination for Medical Reasons has argued that the 22-week time limit is inappropriate in cases of severe foetal impairment, both because pregnant people may not have had access to the necessary diagnostic test before that 'cut-off period', and because parents may require more time to make their decision, following a diagnosis.[139] Limiting the time available in which to make these decisions diminishes their difficulty and the care with which parents make them.

As we noted in Chapter 3, a legally enforced compulsion to continue a non-viable pregnancy may violate the right to freedom from inhuman and degrading treatment,[140] as well as the right to private and family life.[141] International human rights law allows for termination in cases of severe foetal abnormality, without requiring proof that stillbirth or death in the womb is a near certainty.[142] However, the United Nations Committee on the Rights of Persons with Disabilities (UNCRPD) is increasingly resisting legislation that makes it easier to obtain an abortion later in pregnancy in cases of foetal impairment.[143] The Committee's point here is not that such legislation discriminates against

---

[139] See similarly Priaulx, Nicky (note 123), pp 18-19. Routine dating and anomaly scanning is not available across all 19 maternity hospitals in Ireland. HSE, *Creating a Better Future Together: National Maternity Strategy 2016-2020* (2016), p 84; National Maternity Strategy Implementation Plan (2017), comments on Recommendation No 29.

[140] See, for example, *LC v Peru* (note 14); *KL v Peru* (note 14).

[141] *Northern Ireland Human Rights Commission, Re Judicial Review* [2015] NIQB 96 and [2015] NIQB 102.

[142] *Concluding Observations on the Combined Seventh and Eighth Periodic Reports of Peru*, CEDAW/C/PER/CO/7-8 (24 July 2014); Committee on the Elimination of Discrimination against Women, *Concluding Observations on the Fifth and Sixth Periodic Reports of Chile*, CEDAW/C/CHL/CO/5-6 (12 November 2012).

[143] UNCRPD Concluding Observations on the initial report of the United Kingdom CRPD/C/GBR/CO/1; UNCRPD, 'Comments on the draft General Comment No36 of the Human Rights Committee on article 6 of the International Covenant on Civil and Political Rights' www.ohchr.org/Documents/HRBodies/CCPR/GCArticle6/CRPD.docx.

the impaired foetus as a person, or that states are required to protect its life before birth. If the law permits abortion in principle, it cannot forbid it in cases of foetal impairment.[144] In addition, the Committee agrees that abortion must be made available where to refuse it would expose the pregnant person to inhuman and degrading treatment[145] or where a pregnant person was unable to continue a pregnancy for health or socioeconomic reasons after receiving a diagnosis of severe foetal anomaly.[146]

However, the Committee maintains that a specific 'disability exception' within abortion legislation reflects a failure to value disabled people in society. If the law allows the abortion for reasons of disability where it would not otherwise allow abortion at all, it sends the message that disabled life as such is undesirable or unacceptable.[147] In order to address this issue, the Committee has held that states should not legislate to permit abortion for disability-specific reasons in later pregnancy.[148] The Citizens' Assembly's recommendations could fall foul of this position.

There are two ways of trying to ensure that people who receive foetal anomaly diagnoses would be able to access abortion should that be their choice, while bearing the Committee's concerns in mind. The first is to proceed with a foetal anomaly ground regardless of these concerns, but require the legislation to be reviewed for its human rights impact a number of years after its commencement. Such a review clause would require that appropriate data (on access, refusal, grounds and

---

[144] Priaulx, Nicky (note 123), 5; McGuinness, Sheelagh, 'Law Reproduction and Disability: fatally "handicapped"?' (2013) 21(2) *Medical Law Review* 213.

[145] Criminal Code, Chapter 16, §§ 218–219b

[146] Priaulx (note 123), 19.

[147] Garland Thomson, Rosemarie, *Extraordinary Bodies: Figuring Disability in American Culture and Literature* (Columbia University Press, New York 1997) 6.

[148] Committee on the Rights of Persons with Disabilities, Concluding Observations of the Committee on the Rights of Persons with Disabilities Spain, 19–23 September 2011, CRPD/C/ESP/CO/1, [17]-[18].

demographics, for example) be collected so that the operation of the law and in particular its impact on reproductive autonomy could be accurately ascertained and legislative amendments made as appropriate. The second is to interpret the risk to health ground holistically (again in line with the WHO definition) to ensure that abortion is available in appropriate cases of foetal impairment while avoiding the stigmatising impacts of the inclusion of a specific foetal anomaly ground. Germany's law takes this approach, allowing access to abortion where the prospect of continuing the pregnancy in the face of a diagnosis of foetal anomaly poses a grave risk to the woman's mental health.[149] Crucially, this is a 'woman-centred' ground that addresses the pregnant person's current and future suffering, rather than a ground that appears to focus on the condition or perceived worth of the foetus.

Ultimately the decision about which approach would be better is a matter of policy; what is most important is that women in these situations can make a decision about whether to end their pregnancy. At the same time, if the state takes seriously its interest in preserving foetal life, and in improving the lives of people with severe disabilities, it must also recognise that the task of caring for a child or adult with significant health needs should not fall solely to that person's family. Ireland must act to address discriminatory attitudes, or poor-quality information, in abortion decision making. In addition, the government should take extensive educational and socioeconomic measures that support parents voluntarily to continue pregnancies, and ensure a high quality of life for seriously disabled children and adults.[150] This is an extension of the broader argument that the state can best support the continuation of pregnancy by providing positive economic supports. The United Nations Convention on the Rights of Persons with Disabilities requires measures of this kind. Ireland has yet to ratify it.

---

[149] Section 218 Criminal Code.

[150] See further NUI Galway, Centre for Disability Law and Policy, *Submission to the Citizens' Assembly on Repeal of the Eighth Amendment to the Constitution* (2016).

We suggest that the law provide for abortion on grounds of serious or fatal foetal anomaly, without any time limit. Ideally, this should be done under a health ground. Any specific ground should be subject to human-rights-oriented review within a few years of the legislation's commencement.

As a final point, it is crucial to remember disabled pregnant people when we discuss abortion and disability. An exclusive focus on children as the bearers of disability rights infantilises disabled adults. It conceals their equal entitlement to fulfilling sexual and reproductive lives. Punitive laws regulating reproduction – for example on involuntary sterilisation – have disproportionately affected disabled women worldwide. Pregnant people with disabilities will sometimes need abortions for a variety of reasons. Their rights must also be protected.

Risk to life

A great majority of the Assembly voted for abortion to be available where there is a 'real and substantial risk to the life' of the pregnant woman, without any time limit. This recommendation reflects existing constitutional law and legislation in two ways, neither of which has any necessary grounding in law once the 8th Amendment is removed from the Constitution. First, the Assembly voted on risk to life from a physical health condition and from suicide separately. As already noted, this vote conflicts with the Assembly's separate recommendation that abortion legislation should not distinguish between physical and mental health.[151] However, this distinction reflects the PLDPA, which provides separate pathways for suicidal people and people whose life is at risk from physical illness. This distinction has been roundly criticised and

---

[151] In a separate ballot, taken at the request of Assembly members, 72% of the members voted that no distinction should be drawn between the physical and mental health of the woman. Nevertheless, the overall voting pattern indicated a distinction between physical and mental health. No further vote was taken to explore or seek to reconcile these differences.

has no constitutional or other logical basis.[152] Arguably, once the 8th Amendment is removed from the Constitution, the right to equal treatment would mean that requiring people who are suicidal to satisfy a much more onerous procedural 'test' than people with a physical condition that poses a risk to their life is unconstitutional.[153] Second, the Assembly's recommendations use the term 'real and substantial' risk to life. This is an unworkable hangover from the X case that is likely to lead to continued uncertainty in interpreting this ground.

We suggest while it is appropriate to legislate for abortion in cases of risk to life without imposing any term limit, the language and structures of the current law should be changed, and clear and workable language installed in legislation instead.

Conclusion

This chapter makes four key points. First, as far as possible, abortion care provision must facilitate pregnant people's self-determination within non-hierarchical structures. Medical professionals should not be gatekeepers to abortion services, but should be equipped to assist pregnant people to make the best healthcare decisions for them. Grounds-based legislation may undermine that process. These issues can be addressed by encouraging a rights-based approach to interpretation and implementation of grounds-based abortion legislation in practice, but many of the difficulties can be avoided by taking an open, flexible approach to the drafting of grounds. Second, procedural rights must be protected through the development of clear abortion access processes.[154] We must bear in mind that enabling

---

[152] See, for example, Murray, Claire, "Protection of Life during Pregnancy Act 2013': Suicide, Dignity and the Irish Discourse on Abortion' (2016) 25(6) *Social and Legal Studies* 667; de Londras, Fiona, "Suicide and Abortion: Analysing the Legislative Options in Ireland" (2013) 19(1) *Medico-Legal Journal of Ireland*, 4.

[153] Article 40.1, Constitution of Ireland.

[154] Erdman, Joanna, 'The Procedural Turn: Abortion at the European Court of Human Rights' in (eds) Cook, Rebecca, Erdman, Joanna and Dickens,

pregnant people to exercise their reproductive agency is not a matter of removing existing prohibitions on abortion and 'leaving them to it'. Pregnant people must receive the information and support necessary to navigate those processes without fear of delay, misinformation, arbitrary obstruction or intimidation. Third, abortion legislation must be designed with all pregnant people in mind, taking account of the complex and intersecting needs of more vulnerable pregnant people in legislative design. Finally, abortion must be decriminalised.

In the final chapter, we set out some model abortion legislation and explanatory notes that reflect the arguments made in this chapter.

Bernard, *Abortion Law in Transnational Perspective: Cases and Controversies* (University of Pennsylvania Press, 2014), p 121.

5

Model legislation

In this chapter, we outline draft legislation, inspired by the Citizens' Assembly recommendations, but adjusting them where necessary to give effect to pregnant people's rights. The explanatory notes are light; our decisions are explained in more detail in Chapter 4, and we strongly advise that Chapters 4 and 5 are read together. The draft legislation shows that it is possible to design workable legislation that gives meaningful effect to the rights of pregnant people. We build here on previous model drafts that we have worked on with feminist academic colleagues,[1] benefiting from the advice of activists and civil society actors in the process. Of course, as we argued in Chapter 4, legislation alone cannot achieve effective access to abortion care. That requires guidance, principles and an ethic of care that places pregnant women, their views, their opinions and their judgements about what is right for them at its centre. So, any legislation must be supported by rights-supporting interpretative aides and appropriate training. We think that legislation of this kind would make a real difference to pregnant people's lives. To illustrate this, we include

---

[1] Enright, Máiréad et al, 'General Scheme of the Access to Abortion Bill 2015' (2015) 5(1) *feminists@law*; Enright, Máiréad, 'General Scheme of the Reproductive Rights (Northern Ireland) Order 2017' (on file with authors).

case studies, drawing on some stories offered in submissions to the Citizens' Assembly. Although space does not allow for discussion of a comprehensive range of case studies, this selection shows how difficult cases would be addressed both under the current law and under our proposed legislation.

Grounds, time limits, gatekeepers

Our proposal broadly mirrors the legislative recommendations of the Citizens' Assembly. We adopt the same time limits it proposed: 12 weeks, 22 weeks, and no time limit. Gradual restriction in availability of legal abortion as the pregnancy progresses is typically considered a proportionate infringement of the rights of pregnant people, as discussed in Chapter 3, and we suggest that this model is likely to be considered constitutional in Ireland after repeal of the 8th Amendment. Under s. 4(a) of our legislation, until 12 weeks, we propose, as the Assembly did, that abortion should be available without the pregnant person being required to give any reason.[2] We consider the justifications for this approach in Chapter 4.

Between 12 and 22 weeks, the Assembly recommended that the pregnant person should be required to bring her case within one of a range of reasons.[3] As discussed in Chapter 4, however, exceptions-based legislation may carry many serious risks for pregnant people who need abortions. Therefore, in s. 4(b), we show how non-exceptions-based legislation could regulate abortion access in later pregnancy. Our legislation provides that, between 12 and 22 weeks, a doctor would consider a pregnant person's circumstances. However, rather than specify each of the grounds named by the Assembly, we propose a single 'health ground' capable of responding to all of the kinds of case in which the Assembly felt that abortion should be available at this stage in pregnancy. The ground has two parts: first, a medical

---

[2] The Citizens' Assembly, *First Report and Recommendations of the Citizen's Assembly: The Eighth Amendment of the Constitution* (2017).

[3] The Citizens' Assembly (2017), p 12 (see note 2).

practitioner must determine that an abortion is appropriate having regard to the pregnant person's state of health,[4] and second, he or she must take account of the pregnant person's assessment of her own current and future health.

In s. 1 we adopt the World Health Organization definition of 'health'[5] which, as we showed in Chapter 4, is sufficiently broad to allow for a holistic assessment of the pregnant person's physical and mental health and social and economic circumstances, provided those applying the law interpret it in a rights-based manner.[6] It also allows the law to reflect the fact that the same conditions affect pregnant people very differently, depending on their social and economic circumstances.[7] By focusing instead on the potential health consequences of continuation of pregnancy in these circumstances, this approach mitigates some of the risks and harms associated with specifying a rape ground or a serious foetal anomaly ground, which we discussed in Chapter 4.

After 22 weeks, s. 4(c) of our legislation provides for the grounds recommended by the Assembly with some key changes.[8] Unlike the Assembly, and for the reasons explained in Chapter 4, we do not distinguish between risks to physical and mental health. At this point in pregnancy, we also require the authorising practitioner to take into account the pregnant person's views on the impact of continued pregnancy on her current and future health. The legislation does not qualify risk to health with language like 'serious' for the reasons explained in Chapter 4. We trust that medical practice will develop to ensure that abortion after 22 weeks takes place only where health risks are especially serious; that has been the experience in other

---

[4] This is a modification of section 5 of the Abortion Law Reform Act, 2008, Victoria Australia.

[5] Preamble, Constitution of the World Health Organization 14 UNTS 185 (1946).

[6] We discussed the importance of this in Chapter 4.

[7] Peter Boylan, evidence to the Joint Committee on the Eighth Amendment to the Constitution, 18 October 2017.

[8] The Citizens' Assembly (2017), p 12 (see note 2).

jurisdictions, even where there is no specific law, and there is no reason why it would not also be the case in Ireland. The requirement that the risk at this point in pregnancy be a serious one is underlined by the requirement to consult with another practitioner. In addition, the draft legislation does not require that the medical practitioner's decision be taken in 'good faith'. We assume the decriminalisation of abortion, and so this qualification is not necessary.

Finally, unlike the Assembly, and again for reasons discussed in Chapter 4, we do not distinguish between a serious and fatal foetal anomaly ground,[9] and we do not require proof of a 'fatal' diagnosis before a termination can be carried out at this point in pregnancy. We are aware that there are conditions that do not inevitably lead to death in the womb, or during or soon after birth, but that affect a newborn's quality of life so severely that loving parents ought to be supported in deciding to spare them such terrible suffering.[10] Forced continuation of such pregnancies may generate precisely the same violations of pregnant people's human rights experienced in cases of fatal foetal abnormality, so that termination of pregnancy should be made available. Again, we trust medical and parental judgment to restrict the availability of abortions to severe cases.

The Assembly did not specify which, or how many, medical practitioners a pregnant person should consult with before obtaining an abortion. Bearing in mind our discussion in Chapter 4 around the need to protect pregnant people's autonomous decision making, and therefore to avoid burdensome certification processes, we propose that one medical practitioner should suffice to authorise an abortion, and that thought should be given to empowering medical practitioners other than doctors to provide abortion care, and certify abortion access where appropriate. We do not require that abortions take place

---

[9] The Citizens' Assembly (2017) (see note 2).

[10] See Termination for Medical Reasons, *TMFR Ireland Submission to the Citizens' Assembly* (2016). See also Clare Cullen-Delsol, evidence to the Joint Committee on the Eighth Amendment to the Constitution, 25 October 2017.

in specific locations; as outlined in Chapter 4, it should be possible to accommodate a range of locations for abortion care depending on the individual circumstances in a particular case. Under s. 4(c), the authorising practitioner is required to formally consult with a colleague as part of evaluating the pregnant person's case if the pregnancy has passed 22 weeks gestation. The second doctor is not, however, a co-decision maker. Our intention here is to facilitate medical consultation without adding additional cumbersome steps to the decision-making process.

Autonomy and access

The protection and recognition of the rights, autonomy and agency of pregnant people is central to the proposed legislation. This is especially rooted in s. 6. This requires that the law should be interpreted in a way that is 'most favourable to achieving positive health outcomes for the pregnant person and due regard shall be given to the need to respect the rights of the pregnant person to dignity, bodily integrity, privacy and autonomy'. This is modelled on s. 4 of the Mental Health Act 2001, which provides clear direction to government departments, professional regulators, and individual decision makers and practitioners that the law must be interpreted and applied in a rights-based manner. We reinforce this in our model legislation by ensuring that abortions provided under the Act must be voluntary and consensual (s. 6(b)), that pregnant people shall not be *required* to receive directive counselling, read or view images, or undergo a waiting period as a condition of receiving abortion care (s. 6(d)), and that where someone qualifies for abortion care under the Act no procedure or treatment designed to prolong the pregnancy or ensure a live birth is to be undertaken without her consent (s. 6(c)). These provisions are all focused on protecting pregnant people from measures designed to undermine their access to abortion care where they elect to bring their pregnancy to an end, and reflect experience of such measures in other jurisdictions[11] and under the Protection of Life During Pregnancy Act 2013 (PLDPA).[12]

We also include provisions designed to ensure meaningful access to abortion: the complete decriminalisation of abortion (s. 2), a statutory obligation on the Minister for Health to ensure that abortion services are provided in a timely manner (s. 3(1)), a guarantee of non-discrimination in access to abortion care (s. 3(2)), a process to ensure that a pregnant person is enabled to seek a second opinion if refused abortion care (s. 5), a provision to protect medical practitioners' right to conscientious objection but prevent institutions from claiming such an objection (s. 7), a provision to protect people entering and leaving premises where abortion care is provided (s. 8), and a provision requiring the provision of effective and accurate abortion information (s. 9).

As discussed in Chapter 4, in order to ensure that the Oireachtas remains actively engaged with the operation of the legislation, and to create the conditions for comprehensive and effective data gathering around the operation of the law—including situations where access to abortion care is refused—we include in s. 11 a provision requiring a statutory review of the human rights impact and operation of the Act three years after its commencement.[13]

A proposed legislative text

Part 1: Definitions

1. In this legislation:

    a. *appropriately qualified medical practitioner* may include nurses and midwives, as well as doctors, as provided for under regulation;

---

[11] See the discussion in Chapter 4.

[12] See the discussion in Chapter 3.

[13] This is modeled directly on s. 7 of the Gender Recognition Act 2015.

b. *health* means a state of complete physical, mental and socio-cultural wellbeing and not merely the absence of disease or infirmity. It includes sexual and reproductive health;

c. *pregnancy counsellor* means any person or organisation engaging in, or holding himself, herself or itself out as having experience or expertise to engage in, the provision of information, advice or counselling to persons experiencing, or who have experienced, a crisis pregnancy;[14]

d. *pregnant person* includes pregnant minors and all persons who are pregnant regardless of their gender identity.

Part 2: Decriminalisation of abortion

2. Criminal offences

a. Notwithstanding any other provision of law, it shall not be an offence for a pregnant person to self-induce an abortion.

b. Notwithstanding any other provision of law, it shall not be an offence for a pregnant person to consent to or assist in the performance of her own abortion.

c. Notwithstanding any other provision of law, it shall not be an offence for any person to perform or assist in the performance of an abortion with the pregnant person's consent.

d. Section 22 of the Protection of Life During Pregnancy Act 2013 is hereby repealed.

Part 3: Access to abortion

3. Guarantee of access

a. The Minister for Health shall ensure that pregnant persons can obtain safe and timely abortion services in accordance with the provisions of this Act.

---

[14] Definition borrowed from the Health and Social Care Professionals (Amendment) Bill 2016, Republic of Ireland.

b. Access to abortion care and to abortion aftercare shall not be impeded because of the pregnant person's social status, including her race, sex, religion, national or ethnic origin, marital or family status, immigration status, sexual orientation or age.

4. Accessing abortion

a. Abortion before 12 weeks

   i. A person who is not more than 12 weeks pregnant may access abortion on her request without need to show further grounds.

b. Abortion at between 12 and 22 weeks

   i. A person who is more than 12 weeks, but not more than 22 weeks pregnant, may only access an abortion where an appropriately qualified medical practitioner determines that the abortion is appropriate having regard to her state of health.

   ii. In making a determination under this section, the medical practitioner shall have regard, in particular, to the pregnant person's own assessment of her current and future health.

   iii. In making a determination under this section, the medical practitioner shall act with all reasonable haste and communicate the determination to the pregnant person in a timely fashion.

c. Abortion at more than 22 weeks

   i. A person who is more than 22 weeks pregnant may only access an abortion where an appropriately qualified medical practitioner determines that the abortion is appropriate because of:

     1) a risk to the pregnant person's life; or

     2) a risk to the pregnant person's health; or

3) a diagnosis of serious foetal anomaly.

ii. In making a determination under this section, the medical practitioner shall have regard, in particular, to the pregnant person's own assessment of her current and future health.

iii. Otherwise than in cases of imminent risk to the pregnant person's life or health, in making a determination under this section, the medical practitioner must show that he has consulted with another appropriately qualified medical practitioner who agrees that an abortion is appropriate.

iv. In making a determination under this section, the medical practitioner shall act with all reasonable haste and communicate the determination to the pregnant person in a timely fashion.

5. Refusal of care under s. 4

Where an appropriately qualified medical practitioner is of the opinion that a pregnant person who has requested an abortion under s. 4 of this Act is not entitled to access it, he shall:

a. immediately inform her of the refusal;

b. provide written confirmation of the reasons for refusal within 24 hours of refusal;

c. inform her in writing of her entitlement to seek a second opinion, and refer her to an alternative appropriately qualified medical practitioner without delay.

6. Healthcare and self-determination

a. In making any decision under this Act, or in providing abortion care and services, the provisions of the Act shall be interpreted in the manner most favourable to achieving positive health outcomes for the pregnant person and due regard shall be given to the need to respect the rights of the pregnant person to dignity, bodily integrity, privacy and autonomy.

b. No procedure shall be performed on, or treatment administered to, a competent pregnant person under this Act, except with her voluntary and informed consent.

c. Where a pregnant person is entitled to an abortion under s. 4, nothing in this Act shall be read as justifying without the consent of the pregnant person, the performance of another procedure or treatment designed to preserve or prolong the pregnancy, or to ensure a live birth.

d. A pregnant person shall not be required to accept any directive counselling, to read or view any material or images, or to undergo any waiting period, as a condition of receiving abortion care.

Part 4: Protection of abortion access

7. Conscientious objection

a. An appropriately qualified medical practitioner may refuse to participate in the provision of abortion care on the basis of a good faith conscientious objection, except where an abortion is immediately necessary to save the pregnant person's life, or to prevent severe damage to the pregnant person's health.

b. An appropriately qualified medical practitioner asserting a conscientious objection shall, without delay:

  i. inform the pregnant person of the refusal of care in writing;

  ii. inform the pregnant person of her right to be treated by an alternative practitioner who does not hold the same objection; and

  iii. make such arrangements for the transfer of her care as are necessary for her to access abortion care in a timely manner.

c. Institutions, agencies or organisations may not assert a conscientious objection under this section.

d. Medical practitioners asserting a conscientious objection to participation in abortion care must inform their patients of this objection at the outset of treatment, whether by a prominently displayed notice or by other appropriate means.

e. In any legal proceedings arising from this section, the burden of establishing a conscientious objection shall rest on the person seeking to rely on it.

8. Protecting premises[15]

a. A person must not engage in prohibited behaviour within a radius of 100 metres from the perimeter of any premises at which abortions are provided.

b. In this section 'prohibited behaviour' means:

  i. in relation to a person: besetting, harassing, intimidating, interfering with, threatening, hindering, obstructing or impeding that person; or

  ii. threatening behaviour that can be seen or heard by a person accessing, or attempting to access premises at which abortions are provided; or

  iii. recording a person accessing, or attempting to access premises at which abortions are provided without that person's consent, or publishing or distributing a recording so obtained, except in discharge of police duty.

c. Conviction for an offence of engaging in prohibited behaviour under this section shall carry a penalty of a fine not exceeding €2,500, or imprisonment for a term not exceeding 12 months, or both.

d. All necessary police powers of detention and seizure are hereby provided for.

---

[15] This section is partly based on section 9 of the Reproductive Health (Access to Terminations) Act 2013, Tasmania.

9. Misleading abortion information[16]

    a. A pregnancy counsellor shall not publish, distribute, display or broadcast any material likely to mislead or deceive a person who is accessing or attempting to access an abortion.

    b. A pregnancy counsellor that does not provide referrals for abortion care must include in any website, advertising or notification material a statement clearly establishing that it does not provide referrals for abortion care.

    c. Failure to comply with the requirements of ss. 9(a) and 9(b) of this Act shall constitute an offence under this section, carrying a penalty of a fine not exceeding €2500, or imprisonment for a term not exceeding 12 months, or both.

    d. The Minister for Health shall ensure the publication of accessible, impartial and accurate factual information on abortion care, and shall ensure that pregnant persons have timely access to such information on request.

    e. A pregnancy counsellor convicted of an offence under s. 9 (a) or (b) shall not receive state funding, until such time as it can demonstrate compliance with those statutory requirements.

    f. All necessary police powers of detention and seizure are hereby provided for.

10. Code of practice

    a. The Minister for Health shall cause to be prepared, after consultation with such bodies as he considers appropriate, a code or codes of practice for personnel working in abortion care.

    b. The code and codes of practice shall provide, in particular, for specific care pathways for pregnant persons who may face obstacles in accessing abortion care because of their age, social origin, physical or intellectual disability, health condition,

---

[16] This section is partly based on the Pregnancy Counselling (Truth in Advertising) Bill, 2006 (Australia).

educational background, family status, immigration status, or status as a victim of crime.

11. Review of operation of Act

The Minister for Health shall:

a. not later than three years after this section comes into operation, commence a review of the operation of this Act and of the code of practice under s. 10; and

b. not later than 12 months after its commencement, make a report to each House of the Oireachtas of the findings made on the review and of the conclusions drawn from the findings.

Case studies: the proposed law in practice

In this section we illustrate the operation of s. 4 with a selection of case studies. Each case study compares the current Irish law on abortion with the legislation we have proposed.[17]

Róisín's case

Twenty-two weeks into her first pregnancy, Róisín begins experiencing terrible headaches. She attends the emergency room of her local maternity hospital. Her blood pressure is found to be dangerously high, and she has already suffered liver and kidney damage. Severe early onset pre-eclampsia is diagnosed. She is at serious risk of stroke and seizures, and there is a significant associated risk of death. Her doctors have spent three days trying to lower her blood pressure and prevent seizures, but it cannot be controlled. The foetus is alive, but not viable.

---

[17] These case studies are all loosely based on stories of real pregnancies that are already in the public domain; www.abortionrightscampaign.ie/tag/citizens-assembly; www.amnestyusa.org/pdfs/Ireland_She_Is_Not_A_Criminal.pdf; www.ifpa.ie/sites/default/files/documents/media/publications/irish_journey. pdf; www.citizensassembly.ie/en/Meetings/Protection-of-Life-During-Pregnancy-Act-2013-John-Higgins.pdf.

Under the PLDPA

Róisín may be entitled to have birth induced early under the PLDPA because her life is at risk; however, it is not clear at which point in this case her right of access is established. Two obstetricians must be satisfied first that the risk of loss of her life from the pre-eclampsia has become 'real and substantial', and second that this risk can only be averted by the termination of the pregnancy and cannot be averted by the other methods they have been trying. Róisín's doctors must also have regard to the need to preserve unborn human life as far as practicable. The obligation to preserve unborn human life may also be read as meaning that they must try to use other methods to maintain the pregnancy for as long as the foetus' heart is beating, despite the risk to Róisín's health and life. Unlike a case of inevitable miscarriage, it is not clear that this treatment is futile. So, doctors cannot intervene until the foetus' heart stops beating or until Róisín's health deteriorates further so that her life is at 'real and substantial risk'. The PLDPA does not require doctors to take account of Róisín's own views in deciding whether the pregnancy can be terminated.

Under the proposed law

Róisín would be entitled to an abortion under s. 4(c) if one doctor determined and a second agreed that it was appropriate on grounds of risk to her health. Although of course Róisín would not be required to decide there and then, she would be entitled to access abortion care as soon as she wished and the physicians would not have to wait for a risk to life to materialise. In deciding on the appropriateness of a termination, the physician would be required to take account of Róisín's own assessment of her position: if she did not want to run the risk of waiting any longer because of her views of the potential impact on her health, this should carry significant weight in the medical assessment of the appropriateness of making abortion care available.

Cathy's case

Cathy, who is 40, has severe chronic depression and anxiety, which she manages with medication. She has had several suicidal episodes since her teens, and in her thirties was hospitalised for a protracted period. She became severely distressed when she discovered three weeks ago that she was pregnant, and her first instinct was to attempt suicide. She has been in a casual relationship with Tom for a short while, but she does not know how far into her pregnancy she is. Three days ago, Tom interrupted Cathy during what he believes was an attempt to hang herself. Cathy is refusing to see a doctor.

Under the PLDPA

Cathy may be able to access an abortion under the PLDPA, on grounds of risk to life from suicide. Two obstetricians and a psychiatrist would be required to assess her case, which may cause delays, given the shortage of appropriately qualified practitioners in Ireland. However, only one woman was granted a termination on this ground last year and it is not clear how Cathy could 'prove' a sufficient risk of suicide and whether one suicide attempt would be 'sufficient'.[18] It is not clear how far Cathy's pregnancy has progressed. If it is close to viability, the Act may require Cathy's doctors to take measures to give the foetus the best chance of live birth. These may include detention[19] and compulsory medical treatment. The long-term risks of such measures to Cathy's health are not relevant to the statutory analysis. Given this, and Cathy's current health, experience suggests she will bypass the Irish legislation completely and travel to access abortion if she has sufficient resources.[20]

---

[18] Veronica O'Keane, evidence to the Joint Committee on the Eighth Amendment to the Constitution, 25 October 2017.

[19] *HSE v BS* [2017] IEDC 18 indicates that a request under the PLDPA may place a woman at risk of detention under the Mental Health Act 2001.

[20] Murray, Claire, 'The Protection of Life During Pregnancy Act 2013: Suicide, Dignity and the Irish discourse on abortion' (2013) 25(6) *Social and Legal Studies* 667; Peter Boylan, evidence to the Joint Committee on the Eighth Amendment to the Constitution, 18 October 2016.

Under the proposed law

Cathy is entitled to access an abortion under s. 4. The process for access will vary depending on how far the pregnancy has progressed. However, even if the pregnancy has advanced past 22 weeks, she may access an abortion under s. 4(c) if one doctor determines and a second agrees that an abortion is appropriate because her mental health is at risk. There would not be any legal need to determine whether the risk to her health had become a risk to her life, or to delay treatment accordingly. Such an interpretation of the legislation would not be most favourable to achieving positive health outcomes for her under s. 6. In deciding on the appropriateness of a termination, a practitioner would be required to take account of Cathy's own assessment of her position. Finally, under s. 6, Cathy could not be subjected to any non-consensual or coerced treatment designed to prolong the pregnancy.

Nuala's case

This is Nuala's second pregnancy. She is now 16 weeks pregnant. The pregnancy was planned. She was diagnosed with hyperemesis gravidarium early in the pregnancy. Nuala has crippling nausea most of the time and vomits up to 50 times a day. The nausea means that she now struggles to stand or walk. She is unable to look after herself and relies on her husband for everyday care, and to care for their toddler Molly. Nuala has been hospitalised several times for severe dehydration, and has been advised that, later in the pregnancy, it may be necessary to admit her to hospital full-time until the birth in order to manage her condition. Nuala has become very depressed and despondent and is terrified at the thought of labour. Nuala was similarly ill during her first pregnancy. While she continued that pregnancy, and adores Molly, she does not think that she can go through the same process again.

Under the PLDPA

Nuala is not entitled to a termination under the PLDPA because her life is not at risk. If she is not in any condition to travel, she will not be able to access an abortion abroad. Because she is over 12 weeks pregnant, a self-induced abortion with pills,[21] even if it were legal, is inappropriate: it is essentially an induction of labour, which she should not attempt at home.[22] The current Irish abortion law does not provide a solution for Nuala.

Under the proposed law

Nuala would be entitled to a termination before 22 weeks under s. 4(b) if one appropriately qualified medical practitioner deemed it appropriate having regard to her state of health. In making that assessment, the medic may have regard to Nuala's social and economic as well as strictly medical circumstances in determining the impact of continued pregnancy on her health. It is understandable that a person in Nuala's situation might wait, in an effort to determine whether she can cope with the illness until it is safe for the baby to be born. Under the proposed legislation, if it became necessary to terminate later in the pregnancy, Nuala would be permitted to do so under s. 4(c) provided a medical practitioner determined, and a second agreed, that the abortion was appropriate because of the combined risk the pregnancy poses to her physical or mental health. Again, in making this decision, Nuala's views would have to be taken into account, as well as the need to interpret the Act in the manner most favourable to achieving positive health outcomes under s. 6. The same section also means that Nuala could not be subjected to any non-consensual or coerced treatment designed to prolong the pregnancy.

Laura's case

Ten weeks ago, Laura, who is 27, attended a cousin's engagement party at a country hotel. Towards the end of the party, her old friend Sam invited her to go

---

[21] Sheldon, Sally, 'How Can a State Control Swallowing? The Home Use of Abortion Pills in Ireland' (2016) 24 *Reproductive Health Matters* 90.

[22] Women on Waves, 'I've been Pregnant for More than 12 Weeks. Can I Still Use Misoprostol?', available at www.womenonwaves.org/en/page/1031/i-ve-been-pregnant-for-more-than-12-weeks--can-i-still-use-misoprostol.

for a walk with him. When they were isolated from the main group, Sam raped Laura. Laura was devastated. She did not feel able to tell anybody about the rape, especially since she and Sam have many friends in common. No pharmacies were open in the rural area where they were staying, but Laura managed to get the morning after pill on her return to the city a day later. The morning after pill did not work, and some weeks later Laura took a pregnancy test, which was positive. Laura cannot cope with the thought of continuing with the pregnancy because of its association with the rape. She also finds it impossible to speak to anyone about what has happened to her.

Under the PLDPA

Laura is not entitled to a termination under the PLDPA because her life is not currently at risk. If she is not in any condition to travel, she will not be able to access an abortion abroad. Assuming she is not over 12 weeks pregnant, a self-induced abortion with pills may be appropriate, but of course, this is also illegal under Irish law. The current Irish abortion law does not provide a solution for Laura except insofar as the 13th Amendment permits her to travel abroad.

Under the proposed law

The solutions available to Laura under the proposed legislation will vary according to how far her pregnancy has progressed. Laura will not be required to report the rape to anyone within the criminal justice system as a condition of accessing an abortion. If Laura is less than 12 weeks pregnant, she may access an abortion on request under s. 4(a) without disclosing any reason to the person providing the abortion. If the pregnancy has progressed beyond 12 weeks, she can access an abortion under s. 4(b) provided a medical practitioner determines that it is appropriate having regard to her state of health. In making this decision, regard must be had to Laura's assessment of her current and future health. The statutory definition of health here is wide enough to encompass the effects of rape and forced continuation of the resulting pregnancy on Laura's mental health. Similarly, if the pregnancy has progressed beyond 22 weeks, Laura may able to access an abortion on health grounds under s. 4(c); again, the statutory definition of 'health' is wide enough to encompass the effects of rape and forced continuation of the resulting pregnancy on her mental health. Throughout the process, Laura will only be required to see one doctor, although if she does so after 22 weeks, that practitioner will need to consult with another medical practitioner who must agree that abortion is appropriate. This preserves Laura's privacy, and should allow her to choose a practitioner with whom she is comfortable—her GP, for example, or a doctor recommended by a rape crisis centre.[23]

Susie's case

Susie is 19. She is a university student in Limerick, and travels to college from her parents' home outside the city every weekday to attend class. Her periods are irregular due to polycystic ovary syndrome, and she did not suspect that she might be pregnant for some time. Although she had no symptoms of pregnancy, she became worried when she missed a second period. She took a pregnancy test at home during the Christmas holidays, and the result was positive, but she decided to wait until she had returned to university to see a doctor there. It took four days to get an appointment. Susie was shocked to discover that she is already 12 weeks pregnant. She has no savings. She has never travelled outside of Ireland on her own before. She has no idea about how to arrange an abortion abroad. When she asked the university clinic doctor for assistance, he was very unhelpful and reminded her that abortion is illegal in Ireland. She has come across some information online that suggests that abortion is dangerous to women's mental health and will increase her cancer risk in future. Her parents are very controlling, and would not be supportive of her decision to have an abortion.

Under the PLDPA

Susie is not entitled to a termination under the PLDPA because her life is not currently at risk. Because she is already 12 weeks pregnant, a

---

[23] Noeline Blackwell, evidence to the Joint Committee on the Eighth Amendment to the Constitution, 25 October 2017.

self-induced abortion with pills may not be appropriate.[24] That being the case, Susie may need to travel for an abortion. Susie's case illustrates many of the difficulties that arise when women do not have timely access to reproductive healthcare and accurate abortion information in a non-judgmental setting. She will need to research her options, arrange travel and book the treatment for herself. Abortion travel is expensive, practically difficult and emotionally very burdensome, even though Susie is otherwise healthy. Susie may be compelled to disclose her pregnancy and her intended abortion to her parents, at some cost to her privacy and wellbeing. She may be able to access financial support through a charity such as the Abortion Support Network, if she is aware of it. If she struggles to raise the money for the procedure, she may end up accessing her abortion quite late in the pregnancy (up to 24 weeks if she travels to England), or may be compelled to remain pregnant to term. If she travels, she may decide to return soon after the procedure to save on costs, and this will add to the distress of her journey.

Under the proposed law

Susie's case illustrates the importance of flexibility around time limits. She was late in discovering her pregnancy due to circumstances beyond her control. A 14-week time limit for abortion on request under the proposed legislation (rather than a tighter 10- or 12-week limit) would mean that Susie could still access an abortion under s. 4(a) without providing reasons. Even so, Susie would be able to request an abortion under s. 4(b), once a single doctor had assessed her health, taking account of her own perception of the impact of continued pregnancy on her health. Susie's experience of abortion care would be very different under the proposed legislation. She could access it locally with appropriate medical supervision, without the need to travel

---

[24] Women on Waves, 'I've been Pregnant for More than 12 Weeks. Can I Still Use Misoprostol?', available at www.womenonwaves.org/en/page/1031/i-ve-been-pregnant-for-more-than-12-weeks--can-i-still-use-misoprostol.

long distances. A doctor could not comply with this law simply by dismissing her abortion request. The government would be empowered to regulate websites providing misleading abortion information, and would be compelled to ensure that accurate information was published and distributed widely. If abortion were funded in the same manner as other healthcare in pregnancy, Susie's finances would no longer be a serious obstacle to abortion access. Consistent with her right to privacy, she would not be required to disclose her decision to her parents.

Dearbhla's case

Dearbhla is 32. She and her husband Harry married five years ago and she is pregnant with their second child. Their daughter Nora is two. There is a history of Tay Sachs disease in the Harry's family, and so the couple went for genetic counselling some weeks into the pregnancy. Blood and DNA tests showed that both Dearbhla and Harry were carriers. At 16 weeks, Dearbhla had an amniocentesis, which confirmed that the baby would be born with Tay Sachs. The couple were very distressed by this news. Babies with Tay Sachs, if carried to full term, will generally die a painful death before the age of four. Dearbhla is now 20 weeks pregnant.

Under the PLDPA

It is not possible for Dearbhla to access an abortion under the PLDPA because her life is not at risk. She can continue with the pregnancy in Ireland, or travel to the UK for a termination. It is important to note that parents often do not find out about serious foetal anomalies until much later in the pregnancy, due to uneven availability of diagnostic tests. Dearbhla will be able to access a termination in the UK up to, or after, 24 weeks. However, a termination abroad can be traumatic for parents, because, as discussed in Chapter 4, it entails separation from family members, disruption of the grieving process, and the additional stress of travel.

Under the proposed law

Dearbhla would be able to access an abortion if one medical practitioner agreed that a termination was appropriate having regard to her state of health. It is important that grieving parents are given time to make their decision. If Dearbhla wants to wait longer to make her decision, she will still be able to access an abortion after 22 weeks on grounds of serious foetal anomaly, with the agreement of one further medical practitioner. Whether an individual diagnosis comes within the scope of 'serious foetal anomaly' will depend on the circumstances, and should be a medical decision. However, in all cases covered under this legislation, the law should take account of the effects of continuing the pregnancy on the individual pregnant person. The deciding medical practitioner would be required to evaluate Dearbhla's own assessment of her current and future health, consistent with respect for her self-determination. The statutory definition of health here is broad enough to allow him to take account both of her distress and informed judgement around the foetus' quality of life and her assessment of the best interests of her existing child. The same section of the legislation would be used if Dearbhla's foetus were diagnosed with a fatal anomaly.

6

Conclusion

For more than 30 years, women in Ireland have made and been denied reproductive choices under the shadow of the 8th Amendment. In this book, we have shown that this provision was designed precisely to deny reproductive autonomy and to freeze at a particular, illiberal time in Irish politics the ability of women to exercise control over their reproductive lives, of legislators to make law and policy on abortion, and of doctors to provide abortion care in accordance with their consciences, ethics and perceptions of patients' best interests.

In the intervening 34 years, much has changed. The 8th Amendment now looks a relic when read against the backdrop of international human rights law, international best medical practice, and societal attitudes to sexuality, reproduction and choice in Ireland.

In this book, we have shown how a rights-based, agency-centred approach to the Constitution, to legislation, and to the relationship between doctors and patients can help to reinscribe constitutional rights and reproductive autonomy on experiences of pregnancy in Ireland. We have shown not only that making such law is possible and practicable, but also that it will be transformative only if it is accompanied by a shift in practical, political and legal disposition. This requires a rights-based approach to interpretation and application by medical practitioners, lawyers and courts, and a willingness by parliamentarians and courts to approach the regulation of abortion with a commitment to constitutionalism that recognises societal change, takes comparative experience and evidence seriously, and abandons the futile and potentially dangerous search for unattainable legal certainty.

Repeal of the 8th Amendment is a necessary but insufficient step towards the restructuring of pregnancy in Ireland as a fulfilling, empowering and emancipatory experience, whether one continues or ends one's pregnancy, and regardless of the reasons for doing either.

Bibliography

Aiken, Abigail et al, 'Experiences and Characteristics of Women Seeking and Completing At-home Medical Termination of Pregnancy through Online Telemedicine in Ireland and Northern Ireland: A Population-based Analysis' (2017) 124(8) *British Journal of Obstetrics and Gynaecology* 1208.

Berer, Marge, 'Provision of Abortion by Mid-level Providers: International Policy, Practice and Perspectives' (2009) 87(1) *Bulletin of the World Health Organization* 58.

Berer, Marge, 'Abortion Law and Policy Around the World: in Search of Decriminalization' (2017) 19(1) *Health and Human Rights* 13.

Brown, Wendy, 'Reproductive Freedom and the Right to Privacy: A Paradox for Feminists', in Diamond, Irene (ed) *Families, Politics and Public Policy* (1983, Longman).

Brown, Wendy, 'Suffering Rights as Paradoxes' (2000) 7(2) *Constellations* 208.

Chang, Ruth, 'Hard Choices' (2017) 92 *APA Journal of Philosophy* 586.

Connolly, Linda, *The Irish Women's Movement: From Revolution to Devolution* (2001, Springer).

Cook, Rebecca and Dickens, Bernard, 'Abortion Laws in African Commonwealth Countries' (1981) 25(2) *Journal of African Law* 60.

Cornell, Drucilla, 'Dismembered Selves and Wandering Wombs', in Brown, Wendy and Halley, Janet (eds) *Introduction to Left Legalism/Left Critique* (2002, Duke University Press).

Crutcher, Mark, *Firestorm: A Guerrilla Tactic for a Pro-Life America* (1992, Life Dynamics).

Culhane, Leah, 'Reproductive Justice and the Irish Context: Towards an Egalitarian Framing of Abortion', in Quilty, Aideen et al (eds) *The Abortion Papers Ireland: Volume 2* (2015, Cork University Press).

de Londras, Fiona, "An Abortion Law Immune from Constitutional Review?", Human Rights in Ireland, 28 September 2017, available at http://humanrights.ie/constitution-of-ireland/an-abortion-law-immune-from-constitutional-review.

de Londras, Fiona, 'In Defence of Judicial Innovation and Constitutional Evolution', in Cahillane, Laura et al (eds) *Judges, Politics and the Irish Constitution* (2016, Manchester University Press).

de Londras, Fiona, 'Suicide and Abortion: Analysing the Legislative Options in Ireland' (2013) 19(1) *Medico-Legal Journal of Ireland* 4.

de Londras, Fiona and Gwynn Morgan, David, 'Constitutional Amendment in Ireland', in Contiades, Xenephon (ed) *Engineering Constitutional Change: A Comparative Perspective on Europe, Canada and the USA*, (2012, Routledge).

de Londras, Fiona and Kelly, Cliona, *The European Convention on Human Rights Act: Operation, Impact and Analysis* (2010; Round Hall/Thompson Reuters)

Enright, Mairead et al "Abortion Law in Ireland: A Model for Change" (2015) 5(1) *feminists@law*

Enright, Máiréad, General Scheme of the Reproductive Rights (Northern Ireland) Order 2017 (on file with authors).

Enright, Máiréad, "Ireland, Symphysiotomy and UNHRC", Inherently Human, 21 July 2014

Enright, Máiréad and Cloatre, Emile, '*McGee v Attorney General*: Commentary', in Enright, Máiréad et al (eds) *Northern/Irish Feminist Judgments: Judges' Troubles and the Gendered Politics of Identity* (2017, Hart/Bloomsbury Publishing).

Enright, Máiréad, 'The Rights of the Unborn: A Troubling Decision from the High Court', 10 August 2016, Human Rights in Ireland.

Enright, Máiréad, 'Strike for Repeal'. Critical Legal Thinking, 8 March 2017.

Enright, Máiréad, 'Why Would Any Country Put Abortion in the Constitution?', Human Rights in Ireland, 20 April 2017

Erdman, Joanna, 'A Constitutional Future for Abortion Rights in Canada' (2017) 54(3) *Alberta Law Review* 727

Erdman, Joanna, 'Procedural Turn in Transnational Abortion Law' (2010) 104 *American Society of International Law Proceedings* 377.

Erdman, Joanna, 'The global abortion policies database—legal knowledge as a health intervention', 1 November 2017, *The BMJ Opinion.*

Erdman, Joanna, 'The Politics of Global Abortion Rights' (2016) 22(2) *Brown Journal of World Affairs* 39.

Erdman, Joanna, 'The Procedural Turn: Abortion at the European Court of Human Rights', in Cook, Rebecca at al (eds) *Abortion Law in Transnational Perspective: Cases and Controversies* (2014, University of Pennsylvania Press).

Fine, Johanna et al, 'The Role of International Human Rights Norms in the Liberalization of Abortion Laws Globally' (2017) 19(1) *Health and Human Rights* 69.

Fletcher, Ruth, 'Postcolonial Fragments: Representations of Abortion in Irish Law and Politics' (2001) 28(4) *Journal of Law and Society* 568.

Fletcher, Ruth, 'Reproducing Irishness: Race, Gender and Abortion Law' (2005) 17 *Canadian Journal of Women and the Law* 365.

Fletcher, Ruth, 'Contextualising the Canadian Model: A Commentary' Coalition to Repeal the Eighth, 6 December 2016

Fletcher, Ruth, 'Negotiating Strangeness on the Abortion Trail', in Harding, Rosie et al (eds) *Revaluing Care in Theory, Law, and Policy: Cycles and Connections* (2017, Routledge).

Fletcher, Ruth, 'Conscientious Objection, Harm Reduction and Abortion Care', in Donnelly, Mary and Murray, Claire (eds) *Ethical, Legal Ethical and Legal Debates in Irish Healthcare: Confronting Complexities* (2016, Manchester University Press).

Fletcher, Ruth, 'Contesting the Cruel Treatment of Abortion-Seeking Women' (2014) 22(44) *Reproductive Health Matters* 10.

Fletcher, Ruth, 'Judgment: *Attorney General v X*', in Enright, Máiréad et al (eds) *Northern/Irish Feminist Judgments: Judges' Troubles and the Gendered Politics of Identity* (2017, Hart/Bloomsbury Publishing).

Foley, Brian, *Deference and the Presumption of Constitutionality* (2008, IPA).

Fredman, Sandra, 'Foreign fads or fashions: the role of comparativism in human rights law' (2015) 64 *International and Comparative Law Quarterly* 631.

Garland Thomson, Rosemarie, *Extraordinary Bodies: Figuring Disability in American Culture and Literature* (1997, Columbia University Press).

Greasley, Kate, *Arguments about Abortion: Personhood, Morality and Law* (OUP Oxford: 2017)

Hanafin, Patrick 'Valorising the Virtual Citizen: The Sacrificial Grounds of Postcolonial Citizenship in Ireland' (2003) 1 Law, *Social Justice and Global Development*, http://elj.warwick.ac.uk/global/03-1/hanafin.html

Hervey, Tamara and Sheldon, Sally, "Abortion by Telemedicine in Northern Ireland: Patient and Professional Rights across Borders" (2017) 68(1) *Northern Ireland Legal Quarterly* 1

Hoctor, Leah and Lamackova, Adriana, "Mandatory Waiting Periods and Biased Abortion Counseling in Central and Eastern Europe" (2017) 139 *International Journal of Gynecology and Obstetrics* 253.

Hogan, Gerard and Whyte, Gerard, *JM Kelly: The Irish Constitution* (4th edn) (2003, Bloomsbury Professional).

Hug, Chrystel, *The Politics of Sexual Morality in Ireland* (2016, Springer).

Kumar, Anurdha et al, 'Conceptualising Abortion Stigma' (2009) 11(6) *Culture Health and Sexuality* 625

Madden, Deirdre, *Medicine, Law and Ethics*, 3rd Ed. (2016, Dublin; Bloomsbury Professional)

Manning, Edel et al, *Severe Maternal Morbidity in Ireland: Annual Report 2014* (2017; National Perinatal Epidemiology Centre)

Marzilli, Alan, *Fetal Rights* (Chelsea House Publishers: 2005)

Mavronicola, Natasa, 'Is the prohibition Against Torture and Cruel, Inhuman and Degrading Treatment Absolute in International Human Rights Law? A Reply to Steven Greer' (2017) 17(3) *Human Rights Law Review* 479.

McAvoy, Sandra, 'Vindicating women's rights in a foetocentric state: the longest Irish journey' in Giffney, Noreen and Shildrick, Margrit (eds) *Theory on the Edge* (2013, Palgrave Macmillan).

McGuinness, Sheelagh, 'Law Reproduction and Disability: fatally "handicapped"?' (2013) 21(2) *Medical Law Review* 213

McGuinness, Sheelagh, "A Guerilla Strategy for a Pro-Life England" (2015) 7(2) *Journal of Information Law and Technology* 283

McGuinness, Sheelagh, 'Commentary on *Attorney General v X*', in Enright, Máiréad et al (eds) *Northern/Irish Feminist Judgments: Judges' Troubles and the Gendered Politics of Identity* (2017, Hart/Bloomsbury Publishing).

McGuinness, Sheelagh and Widdows, Heather "Access to basic reproductive rights: Global Challenges" in Francis, Leslie (ed), *The Oxford Handbook of Reproductive Ethics* (OUP 2016).

McNeilly, Kathryn, 'From the Right to Life to the Right to Livability: Radically Reapproaching 'Life' in Human Rights Politics' (2015) 41(1) Australian Feminist Law Journal, 141

Menon, Nivedita, 'The Impossibility of Justice: Female Foeticide and Feminist Discourse on Abortion' (1995) 29(1-2) *Contributions to Indian Sociology* 370.

Murphy Lawless, Jo, 'Embodied Truths: Women's Struggle for Voice and Wellbeing in Irish Maternity Services', in Quilty, Aideen et al (eds) *The Abortion Papers Ireland: Volume 2* (2015, Cork University Press).

Murphy, Therese, *Health and Human Rights* (2013; Hart Publishing).

Murray, Claire, "Protection of Life during Pregnancy Act 2013': Suicide, Dignity and the Irish Discourse on Abortion' (2016) 25(6) *Social and Legal Studies* 667

Ngwena, Charles, 'Conscientious Objection to Abortion and Accommodating Women's Reproductive Health Rights: Reflections on a Decision of the Constitutional Court of Colombia from an African Regional Human Rights Perspective' (2014) 58(2) *Journal of African Law* 183

Rebouché, Rachel, 'The Limits of Reproductive Rights in Women's Health' (2011) 63(1) *Alabama Law Review* 1

Rebouché, Rachel, 'Abortion Rights as Human Rights' (2016) 25(6) *Social & Legal Studies* 765.

Rossiter, Ann, *Ireland's Hidden Diaspora: The 'Abortion Trail' and the Making of a London-Irish Underground, 1980-2000* (2009: IASC Publishing)

Sanger, Carol, *About Abortion: Terminating Pregnancy in Twenty-First-Century America*, (Harvard University Press: 2017)

Scott, Rosamund, *Choosing Between Possible Lives: Law and Ethics of Prenatal and Preimplantation Genetic Diagnosis* (Hart Publishing, Oxford 2007)

Sheldon, Sally, 'How Can a State Control Swallowing? The Home Use of Abortion Pills in Ireland' (2016) 24 *Reproductive Health Matters* 90

Sheldon, Sally, 'The Decriminalisation of Abortion: an Argument for Modernisation' (2016) 36(2) *Oxford Journal of Legal Studies* 334

Sheldon, Sally and Fletcher, Joanne, 'Vaccum aspiration for induced abortion could be safely performed by nurses and midwives' (2017) Journal of Family Planning and Reproductive Health Care 1

Sheldon, Sally and Wilkinson, Stephen, 'On the Sharpest Horns of a Dilemma' (2001) 9(3) *Medical Law Review* 201

Sherlock, Leslie, 'Towards a Reproductive Model of Reproductive Justice in Ireland', in Quilty, Aideen et al (eds) *The Abortion Papers Ireland: Volume 2* (2015, Cork University Press).

Sifris, Ronli, 'Restrictive Regulation of Abortion and the Right to Health' (2010) 18 *Medical Law Review*, 185

Smart, Carol, *Feminism and the Power of Law* (1989; Routledge).

Smyth, Lisa, 'Feminism and Abortion Politics: Choice, Rights, and Reproductive Freedom' (2002) 25(3) *Women's Studies International Forum* 335

Trueman, Karen and Magwentshu, Makgoale, 'Abortion in a Progressive Legal Environment: The Need for Vigilance in Protecting and Promoting Access to Safe Abortion Services in South Africa' (2013) 103(3) *American Journal of Public Health* 397

Wade, Katherine, 'Refusal of emergency caesarean section in Ireland: A relational Approach' (2014) 22(1) *Medical Law Review* 1

Wade, Katherine, "Caesarean Section Refusal in the Irish Courts: Health Service Executive v B" (2017) 35(3) *Medical Law Review* 494.

West, Robin, 'From Choice to Reproductive Justice: De-Constitutionalizing Abortion Rights' (2009) 118 Yale Law Journal 1394

Zampas, Christina and Gher, Jaime, 'Abortion as a Human Right – International and Regional Standards' (2008) 8 *Human Rights Law Review* 249

Index